Legends of the Blues

of the

William Stout

Abrams ComicArts, New York

Editors: Sheila Keenan and Charles Kochman
Designer: Sara Corbett
Managing Editor: David Blatty
Production Manager: Alison Gervais

Library of Congress Cataloging-in-Publication Data:

Stout, William, 1949–
  Legends of the blues / by William Stout.
      pages cm
  Includes bibliographical references.
  ISBN 978-1-4197-0686-8
1. Blues musicians—Portraits. I. Title.
  ML87.S89 2013
  781.643092'273—dc23
  [B]

                                2012045834

Printed and bound in China
10 9 8 7 6 5 4 3 2 1

Abrams ComicArts books are available at special discounts when
purchased in quantity for premiums and promotions as well as
fundraising or educational use. Special editions can also be created
to specification. For details, contact specialsales@abramsbooks.com
or the address below.

115 West 18th Street
New York, NY 10011
www.abramsbooks.com

This book is dedicated
to two of the world's
greatest artists:

———————————————

**Willie Dixon &
Robert Crumb**

———————————————

Both are never-ending sources
of insight, inspiration, integrity,
and vision. The works of both
resonate with the rhythms of life,
stir my soul, and bring a satisfied
smile to my lips.

— W. S.

CONTENTS

♫ ♪

GOT THE BLUES

BY ED LEIMBACHER

valon's my home town, always on my mind . . .

A You won't find Mississippi John Hurt among the scores of bluesmen (and women) gathered in this book and rendered so splendidly in water-color portraits by Southern California artist William Stout, but you will find Mississippi Fred McDowell ("I do not play no rock 'n' roll, y'all, I just play the natch'ul blues"), and Sippie Wallace, too. Delta guitar ace Son House isn't here, but the youngster who learned much from him—Robert Johnson—is (and spectacularly so). Georgia twelve-string master and brilliant singer Blind Willie McTell (Bob Dylan got that one right) is similarly absent, but his place has been more-than-adequately filled by Blind Willie Johnson, whose voice is as dark as the Get Right Church basement, and whose guitar slides into truths as substantial as its wooden steeple.

Seasoned fans of the blues or of comics art or of R. Crumb—the always elusive, ever-eclectic artist extraordinaire—likely know that the missing musi-cians mentioned above do appear in the series of old-time-blues and jug-band-folk figures painted by Crumb three decades ago, seen first on trading cards, then eventually as part of the Abrams book titled *R. Crumb's Heroes of Blues, Jazz & Country*. When popular demand for other blues figures warranted a second, more extensive series to include women, later musicians, and the post-war Chicago blues scene in particular, Crumb was happy to pass the torch to his younger compadre, the equally eclectic Bill Stout.

Now as I was a-motorvatin' back into town, saw a Cadillac sign sayin' "No Money Down" . . .

When I first met Bill at the E.C. Comics Convention in New York City four decades ago, he was a rising star in the comic-strip studios of that time, proudly assisting Russ Manning on *Tarzan* as well as the Harvey Kurtzman–Bill Elder duo tag-teaming "Little Annie Fanny" in *Playboy*. I'd traveled to New York from Seattle as a curious non-fan old enough to have bought such E.C. titles as

Weird Fantasy, *Two-Fisted Tales*, and *MAD* (the color comics version) as a kid. I thought it might be fun to meet and greet the writers and illustrators responsible for creating those pieces of America's pop-culture, melting-pot past.

And it *was*—an affirmation of independence and comics creativity that still took a back seat to this: my brief introduction to illustrator Bill Stout, just ahead of his hurrying off to some meeting, inadvertently leaving his portfolio of samples behind. I had the unearned good fortune to notice the portfolio, claim it in Bill's name, and deliver it to him, once I'd obtained his hotel room number. From that moment of serendipity came our forty-year friendship, which has survived time and distance and the ironic economics of art as we drifted gradually from me buying, even commissioning, works by Stout, to the present day, when "the first Stout collector" can no longer afford to collect Stout. . . . So it was good that we also have had a commonality of interest in the Four Fs—food, film, and the female form—and a passion for record collecting driven in part by our mutual love of the blues.

Gon' t' get up in the mornin', I b'lieve I'll dust my blues . . .

Peruse this book and you'll find Skip James and Elmore James—bluesmen of frail health, taken too soon (Skip, by the way, is one of two players presented by Crumb that Bill chose to picture again; who's the other?); both the Empress of the Blues, Bessie Smith, and the shadowed, little-known belter Bessie Tucker; "Big Boy" Crudup and "Half Pint" Jaxon, the former with two songs recorded by Elvis, the latter mainly forgotten now; the blues anatomized by electric guitarist T-Bone Walker and country bumpkin Hambone Willie Newbern; Jimmys Yancey, McCracklin, Rogers, and Reed (and 'Spoon's here, too); rediscovered great Bukka White, master of anecdotal "sky" songs and chooglin' train songs, welcoming his cousin, the up-and-coming guitarist B.B. King; some urban class, adduced courtesy of Miss Dinah Washington and (made beautiful here) Billie Holiday; plus stylish male vocalists Louis Jordan, Big Joe Williams, and Charles Brown.

And so they continue, portrait by portrait, page by page, past two separate harp aces named Sonny Boy Williamson; a further Chicago contingent comprised of Chess stars Walter, Waters, and Wolf; and also (somebody cue Mr. Jordan) five guys named Slim—blues folk remembered and revitalized, a hundred people portrayed in all, many renowned musicians, a few revered ones, and a handful you've never heard of. But thank Mr. Stout nonetheless for having included them in his splendid homage to the blues.

The blues had a baby, and they named it "rock 'n' roll" . . .

Bill came to the original blues—as created by African Americans—a step at a time via his fascination with the electric bass and his vast collection of records documenting the years of the so-called British Invasion and all the years since, particularly those rock bands that played rhythm 'n' blues: the Rolling Stones, Alexis Koerner, the Yardbirds and spin-offs, the Who, the original Fleetwood Mac and guitarist Peter Green, the incarnations of Eric Clapton, John Mayall, and Long John Baldry, maybe the Pretty Things, too, but assuredly umpteen other groups unknown to me until brought vividly to life by my ratcheted-up, excitable friend (for example, Bill recently got me listening to the blues-flavored duo known as the White Stripes).

Because I'm a few years older, with Southern roots, I came up listening to great radio stations, large or small, broadcasting from Macon and Montgomery, Nashville and New Orleans, and the Tex-Mex border—concentrated periods hearing rockabilly, then rhythm 'n' blues, then the country blues, electrified Chicago blues, and deep soul. From the early sixties to the late seventies I read every blues-related interview, magazine, and book I could lay hands on, in those pre-Internet years; and in 1968–69 I wrote what was apparently the first feature-film script devoted to Delta blues genius Robert Johnson. Bill was one of the first to read the finished script (which circulated for decades, drawing nibbles and letters of intent, meetings and printed excerpts, but which never saw actual production). But beyond Johnson, Bill and I also devoted many phonographic hours to the "Okay, But Have You Heard This One?" listening game, each attempting to stump, top, or "school" the other, and I do hereby attest to having gained new insights into certain musicians, not to mention the art of illustration, while in the pleasant company of Mr. Stout—soon to become your personable traveling guide to the total spectrum of the blues.

Woke up this mornin', feelin' 'round for my shoes, you know I got them old walkin' blues . . .

Enthusiasm, professionalism, and his o'er-vaulting artistry, always set to the highest bar—such are the tools William Stout takes to the studio each day. In a remarkable, awards-rich career, he has ascended from watercolor portrait artist at Disneyland to designer of such worlds for the Disney Imagineers; gone from drawing monsters in fanzines to creating new monsters and weapons and entire production looks, from sets to one-sheet posters, for Hollywood features; mastered a variety of media and used them judiciously, from pen-and-ink sketches for fans to watercolor paintings for his cherished dinosaur projects, from the oil paintings of his compelling popular series on the wildlife of Antarctica to his latest in-demand skills, employing oil paints or whatever else works to execute massive murals on the walls of various natural history museums. (Yes, I have exaggerated the borders and separations among these tasks.) Yet still he finds the time and energy to provide a new cover for a favorite comic book, or design a toy for some start-up dreamer, or maintain the sketches required by his own entrepreneurial publishing company . . . or plan the book he hopes to do next, honoring the best white blues musicians of the past and present.

An excellent idea . . . but maybe before that, the essential, soon-to-be-sought sequel to this gem? Bill ol' pal, there's lots of us already queued up to buy the book that adds your takes on, oh, I don't know, Otis Spann, Magic Sam, Johnny Shines, KoKo Taylor, Peetie Wheatstraw, Buddy Guy (and you can throw in Junior Wells if you want), James Cotton, R. L. Burnside, Hubert Sumlin, Pinetop Perkins, maybe Z. Z. Hill [voice fading out] . . . and Taj . . . [blessed silence . . . then faintly]

Got the blues, can't be satisfied . . .

Ed Leimbacher *is an award-winning writer who owns the Seattle area bookshop MisterE Books. An ace poet, a former* Rolling Stone *magazine scribe, a music-oriented screenwriter, a brilliant author of some of the most clever print and film ads ever made, as well as being an expert on the mystery novel genre, Mr. Leimbacher first met William Stout in 1972.*

DISCOVERING THE BLUES

The American musical form known as the blues is my personal desert-island music, as in the answer to "If I were stranded on a desert island yet somehow could listen to music but were only allowed one genre, what would it be?"

My first scrapes with the blues came in the same bass-ackwards fashion that they did for most white baby boomers: not from its rich African American origins but through the British Invasion of the 1960s. Groups like Manfred Mann, the Rolling Stones, the Yardbirds, Them, and the Animals took our own homegrown American music and dished it right back to us with British flair. Most of us were ignorant of the American sources of their music. It wasn't long, however, before those same groups led grateful legions of us down that righteous path from the blues in its secondhand form to the Real Thing.

In high school I was a huge fan of the blues-influenced English band the Yardbirds. For me, they were *it*. I loved Eric Clapton's intense, blues-based guitar work and the energy and exotic qualities of Jeff Beck's exciting playing. (Jimmy Page had not joined the band at that point.) I had to own every single thing that band recorded.

One day in the supermarket, while perusing the small bin where I usually bought my LPs, I came across a live album by Sonny Boy Williamson and the Yardbirds. That record stopped me in my musical tracks. As far as I knew, this LP wasn't part of the Yardbirds' oeuvre . . . and who was Sonny Boy Williamson?

I bought the record immediately, took it home as fast as I could, and popped it onto my turntable. The music that flowed out of my cheap speakers overwhelmed me with a fantastic sensation. It felt as if I'd come home in a spiritual sense, as if I had found the music that had been lying in wait for me all my short life. These sounds captured my very heart and soul. I didn't know it then, but this music was called the blues.

Not at all disappointed that the LP didn't sound like the Yardbirds, I obtained a tiny inch-and-a-half Hohner harmonica (free with any purchase at a Simi Valley, California, music shop; fifty cents otherwise). I began to imitate Sonny Boy's harp work on that LP, as well as Keith Relf's harmonica parts on the Yardbirds songs.

Eventually I moved up to a Hohner Marine Band and then a Hohner Blues Harp. After years of tearing up my lips on the Hohners, I've become loyal to the exquisitely designed harmonicas from War's skilled harp player, Lee Oskar.

Harmonicas are great. They can easily be taken anywhere. In my hitchhiking days of the 1970s, I'd practice on one between rides. When I left my drum stool and became a frontman, I began to seriously study the harmonica and the way it was played by Keith, Sonny Boy, Paul Jones of Manfred Mann, and, of course, blues great Little Walter (the crisp precision of Paul Butterfield and Stevie Wonder was—and is—beyond me).

Going to live blues concerts by B.B. King and Peter Green's Fleetwood Mac in particular cemented my heavy love for this vital genre of music. Over time I branched out with my blues listening and built up a sizable library of what I considered the finest blues recordings. I was knocked out when Robert Crumb released his blues trading card set, *Heroes of the Blues*, in 1980. Robert's expressive drawings, as usual, were so heartfelt. They were a wonderful way of communicating his love for that music and those musicians.

The U.S. government declared 2003 the official "Year of the Blues." As a result, Shout! Factory, an entertainment company formed by my friend Richard Foos, a fellow blues fan, a black music champion, and the cofounder of Rhino Records, decided to release a series of "best of" CDs by prominent American blues artists. Shout! licensed the blues trading card images from Robert Crumb to use on its CD covers. But there were some musicians that Robert hadn't drawn for his card set. Despite the record company's request, he didn't want to produce any new blues art for Shout!

I was called and asked if I could draw Ma Rainey, Mississippi Fred McDowell, and J. B. Lenoir in the same format as the Crumb cards. I agreed. Combining two of my great loves—drawing and the blues—turned out to be one of the most enjoyable jobs of my career.

After I completed the CD art, I didn't want to stop, so I drew Robert Johnson, a favorite bluesman of mine missing from Robert's card set. Not too long after drawing Mr. Johnson, I was diagnosed with prostate cancer. Following my surgery, I was in recovery for two months and forced to sit around. Never one to be idle, I made a list of my favorite old blues guys and gals whom Robert hadn't drawn. Fortunately for me, his preferences were for the really old players and singers. He hadn't touched the later artists, the musicians I was nuts about, like Chess and Checker Records artists Muddy Waters, Willie Dixon, Howlin' Wolf, Bo Diddley, and Little Walter. My own field of dreams was wide open.

My list grew to fifty names. I began drawing nonstop. In the middle of this self-imposed labor of love, I thought, "What about the British blues players I love so much?" So I made another list of fifty. Then it occurred to me, "Hey! I can't leave out my contemporary American fave raves!" My Legends of the Blues project list now totaled out at 150.

I initially intended for them to be released as three sets of trading cards marking three different eras until my friend Denis Kitchen, the original publisher/instigator of the Crumb cards, proposed that I use them to create a book instead.

ABOUT THE SELECTIONS

Abrams ComicArts agreed to publish the first of my three proposed blues books but asked that I expand the first book from fifty entries to one hundred. I enthusiastically agreed. The blues artists chosen for this book have at least three things in common:

❶ I love and am passionate about their music.

❷ Except for Skip James and Blind Willie Johnson, two bluesmen I just couldn't bear to leave out, none of the artists in this book appear in R. Crumb's *Heroes of the Blues* series.

❸ All the performers in this book were born before 1930.

So, except for not repeating Crumb, my choices were extremely personal.

As such, this is a book that probably won't please blues purists. It will be argued by some that several of my selections are not blues singers or even musicians at all.

Well, sorry.

Several artists in this book have discographies that cover many musical genres. (I don't refer to them as "crossover" artists, because that term is usually applied to black artists who cross over, saleswise, into the white market.) Billie Holiday, for example, sang jazz, blues, and pop, all in her own highly personal style. How in the heck would you truly characterize the wide-ranging music of my late friend Screamin' Jay Hawkins—or the unique oeuvre of Bo Diddley? Even artists who are solidly acknowledged as blues greats, such as John Lee Hooker, seldom worked solely in the classic twelve-bar tradition.

I have always been interested in musical cross-pollination. Such genre mixing often occurred within the African American musical community. When country players met city players, when blues musicians encountered jazz and gospel musicians, when performers from one region jammed with performers from another part of the country, the all-encompassing gumbo of African American music ultimately benefited, dramatically deepening our nation's richly diverse cultural heritage.

I believe that cross-pollination resulted in one of the greatest years in pop music history: 1967. This was a year when pop and rock music were practically devoid of formatting; FM disc jockeys could play whatever they liked. A rock hit could follow a blues song that had just been preceded by the soul tune that came after a jazz number. George Harrison introduced Indian music to a new pop audience and sowed the seeds for the current appreciation of world music. Gram Parsons brought the basics of country music to rock 'n' roll. No one seemed to mind; in fact, as an enthusiastic audience, we music fans celebrated the cross-pollination as much as the musicians who were the first beneficiaries of unprejudiced exposure to different musical cultures. So, this book includes artists who have strayed into musical forms other than the blues. I think each genre ultimately benefited from and informed the others.

My appreciation of musical cross-pollination extends well into my Interesting Covers selections for each artist. Most, but not all, of the cover versions I selected are by rock musicians, many of them British, further reinforcing the blues' contribution to rock music. As the great Muddy Waters sang, "The blues had a baby and they named it rock 'n' roll."

If you are familiar with the legacy of the blues and its greatest practitioners, reading this book will feel like you're spending time with old friends. If you're not aware of the depth and history of this richly entertaining genre, our homegrown creation by African Americans, then prepare yourself for an everlasting treat.

William Stout
Pasadena, California
October 2012

ALBERT AMMONS

MAIN INSTRUMENT: Piano
BORN: Chicago, Illinois; September 23, 1907
DIED: Chicago, Illinois; December 2, 1949

RECOMMENDED TRACKS: "Boogie Woogie Stomp," "Swanee River Boogie," "The Blues"

INTERESTING TRIBUTE: The German pianist Jörg Hegemann honored Ammons on what would have been his one hundredth birthday with the album *A Tribute to Albert Ammons*.

Albert C. Ammons learned piano from his parents and neighbors. He played well by age ten and developed decent blues chops by the time he was twelve. Pine Top Smith personally encouraged the young pianist, whose other main influences were Jimmy Blythe, Jimmy and Alonzo Yancey, and Hersal Thomas.

Ammons met Meade Lux Lewis when they were both teen cabbies. They practiced at the depot during their downtime and publicly played (often together) after their shifts. By 1934 Ammons was leading his own small group at a South Side Chicago club. A powerhouse stride pianist, he became known for his boogie-woogie after his Decca hits "Boogie Woogie Stomp" and the million-selling "Swanee River Boogie," recorded in 1936 under the name Albert Ammons and His Rhythm Kings.

He then moved to New York and played regularly at Café Society with Lewis, as well as with Kansas City pianist Pete Johnson and blues shouter Big Joe Turner. In 1938 the four created a sensation at Carnegie Hall's *From Spirituals to Swing* concert, igniting a nationwide boogie-woogie craze. Albert later performed with Benny Goodman and Harry James. Ammons and Lewis inspired generations of improvisational musicians with their one-day session collaborations on *The First Day* (1939), the initial release of the now-famous jazz label Blue Note.

Ammons recorded several duets with Pete Johnson for RCA Victor Records but ceased playing for three years after accidentally severing a fingertip making a sandwich. He made solo and band records, then performed a duet with Lewis in the Lena Horne film *Boogie-Woogie Dream* (1944). He played regularly in Chicago from 1945 to 1949. He backed Sippie Wallace and collaborated with guitarist Lonnie Johnson as well as with his own son, hard-bop tenor saxophonist Gene Ammons. Always working, Ammons's final performances were on records with Lionel Hampton and at Harry S Truman's second-term inauguration.

TRIVIA: Tragically, both Albert Ammons and his son Gene died while only in their forties (forty-two and forty-nine, respectively).

ALBERT AMMONS

KOKOMO ARNOLD

(JAMES ARNOLD)

MAIN INSTRUMENTS: Slide guitar, vocals
BORN: Lovejoy's Station, Georgia; February 15, 1901
DIED: Chicago, Illinois; November 8, 1968

RECOMMENDED TRACKS: "Milk Cow Blues," "Old Original Kokomo Blues"

INTERESTING COVERS: "Milk Cow Blues" (Aerosmith, Willie Nelson, Robert Johnson as "Milk Cow's Calf Blues," Elvis Presley as "Milk Cow Blues Boogie"), "Old Original Kokomo Blues" (Robert Johnson as "Sweet Home Chicago")

After his cousin taught James Arnold some fundamental guitar, Arnold began his musical career in Buffalo, New York, in the early 1920s while still working as a farmhand and steel worker in Pittsburgh, Pennsylvania. His first recordings were made in Memphis in 1930 as Gitfiddle Jim. In 1929 Arnold moved to Chicago, working as a bootlegger and performing music on the side. The repeal of Prohibition ended his business and Arnold became a full-time musician. This southpaw player's concentrated bottleneck guitar style and brisk blues vocals distinguished him from other players of the time.

"Kokomo" was the subject of Scrapper Blackwell's first recorded blues (1928); the song may have been about Kokomo, Indiana, or a brand of coffee popular in the early twentieth century. Regardless, when James Arnold rearranged Scrapper's song as "Old Original Kokomo Blues" in 1934, he had no idea it would promptly result in his new moniker: Kokomo Arnold.

From 1934 to 1938 Arnold recorded eighty-eight songs for Decca, seven of which are lost. Peetie Wheatstraw played piano on some tracks, but most of Kokomo's records were solo efforts. Wheatstraw, Bumblebee Slim, and Kokomo were Decca's dominant blues sellers in the 1930s. Arnold's reputation as a live performer secured him steady work in Chicago with occasional gigs in New York.

Fed up with the entertainment business, Kokomo quit music in late 1938 to become a Chicago factory worker. Despite his rediscovery by blues researchers in 1962 and the new wave of interest in the blues from young white audiences, Arnold showed little interest in restarting his musical career. He never recorded again and eventually died of a heart attack.

As perhaps two of Robert Johnson's biggest inspirations, Kokomo Arnold and Peetie Wheatstraw were seminal influences on the blues.

TRIVIA: The term "dust my broom," introduced in Kokomo Arnold's "Sagefield Woman Blues," became a Robert Johnson song title and Elmore James's biggest hit.

KOKOMO ARNOLD

FRED BELOW

MAIN INSTRUMENT: Drums
BORN: Chicago, Illinois; September 16, 1926
DIED: Chicago, Illinois; August 14, 1988

RECOMMENDED TRACKS: "School Days" (and most of Chuck Berry's pre-1962 Chess hits), "Off the Wall" (and most of Little Walter's Chess hits)

After playing drums in a high school jazz band, Fred Below studied percussion at the Roy C. Knapp School of Percussion, where he fell in love with bebop. A draftee, he served in the 427th Army Band, playing with Lester Young. Below played in many German nightclubs before returning to Chicago in 1951, where he discovered that the blues had surpassed jazz in popularity.

Muddy Waters's drummer introduced Below to the Three Aces—Junior Wells (vocals, harp), Louis Myers (guitar), and Dave Myers (bass)—although Below's jazz drumming didn't mesh with the Three Aces' Chicago blues sound at first. Below's next break came when Little Walter quit Muddy Waters's band (he was replaced by Junior Wells) to exploit the huge success of Walter's solo hit "Juke." Little Walter and the Nightcats (formerly the Three Aces) became the hottest electric blues band in Chicago.

Below and his bands had an enormous effect on the Chicago music scene, primarily due to the engaging sophistication of Below's drumming. His playing was an integral component of the Chess Records sound, establishing a rhythmical archetype that influenced hundreds of players. He created the standard for the classic blues shuffle beat with his Aces work. Below's followers admire his ride cymbal work, his wood block accents and his trademark tom-tom fills.

In constant demand as a session man, Below played on nearly all of Little Walter's best-known records. In 1955 Below stopped performing live, preferring studio work. A small sample of Fred's session credits reads like a blues who's who: Muddy Waters, Chuck Berry, Otis Rush, Elmore James, Junior Wells, Buddy Guy, Dinah Washington, Bo Diddley, John Lee Hooker, and Howlin' Wolf.

Below and the Myers brothers reformed the Three Aces for one last European tour in 1970. Fred Below died of cancer eighteen years later.

FRED BELOW

CHUCK BERRY

(CHARLES EDWARD ANDERSON BERRY)

MAIN INSTRUMENTS: Guitar, vocals
BORN: St. Louis, Missouri; October 18, 1926

RECOMMENDED TRACKS: "Wee Wee Hours," "Guitar Boogie," "Confessin' the Blues,"
"Time Was," "I've Changed," "Merry Christmas, Baby," "TV Mama," "Childhood
Sweetheart," "It's My Own Business"; *The Chess Box* collects seventy-one great songs.

INTERESTING BLUES COVERS: "Confessin' the Blues" (Rolling Stones), "I'm Talking
About You" (Animals), "Guitar Boogie" (Yardbirds as "Jeff's Boogie")

INTERESTING ROCK COVERS: "Rock 'n' Roll Music" (Beatles, Beach Boys),
"Maybellene" (Foghat), "No Money Down" (Humble Pie), "Too Much Monkey
Business" (Yardbirds), "Reelin' and Rockin'" (Dave Clark Five), "You Can't Catch
Me" (Love Sculpture), "Sweet Little Sixteen" (Animals, Beach Boys as "Surfin'
USA"), "Around and Around" (Animals), "Roll Over Beethoven" (Beatles), "You
Never Can Tell" (EmmyLou Harris), "Little Queenie" (Rolling Stones)

This talented blues artist became far more celebrated as the key innovator of
the blues' world-renowned descendant: rock 'n' roll. He melded country and
western style with blues melodies and twangy guitar to create the distinctive
sound of rock 'n' roll. Chuck Berry was rock's greatest songwriter and one of
its greatest guitarists and performers.

Chuck Berry began performing T-Bone Walker style grandstanding and blues
in his teens, and he first publicly performed while in high school. By 1953 he was
playing mostly blues and ballads (and country music for whites) with the Johnnie
Johnson Trio. Johnson became a longtime collaborator.

In 1955, on Muddy Waters's recommendation, Berry traveled to Chicago.
Chuck thought his blues material would excite Chess Records, but it was his cover
of an old Bob Wills country-and-western song that got Leonard Chess's attention.
"Ida Red," renamed "Maybellene," sold more than a million copies.

After a four-year wane, his popularity surged as British Invasion acts recorded
popular covers of his songs. In 1964, he recorded six hits and appeared with his
U.K. protégés in the Teenage Awards Music International live *TAMI Show*. Berry
left Chess for Mercury, but the hits dried up and he returned to Chess. In 1972, he
achieved his only No. 1 single, "My Ding-a-Ling." Chuck has never stopped touring.

TRIVIA: John Lennon said, "If you tried to give rock and roll another name, you
might call it 'Chuck Berry.'" Taylor Hackford directed the fascinating 1987 Berry
documentary *Hail! Hail! Rock 'n' Roll*.

CHUCK BERRY

BIG MACEO

(MAJOR MERRIWEATHER)

MAIN INSTRUMENTS: Piano, vocals
BORN: Atlanta, Georgia; March 31, 1905
DIED: Chicago, Illinois; February 23, 1953

RECOMMENDED TRACKS: "Chicago Breakdown," "Worried Life Blues," "Texas Stomp," "Detroit Jump"

INTERESTING COVERS: "Worried Life Blues" (Chuck Berry, Animals, Eric Clapton)

A self-taught pianist influenced by the recordings of Leroy Carr, Roosevelt Sykes, Meade Lux Lewis, and Albert Ammons, Major Merriweather's piano skills were well honed by the time he arrived in Detroit in 1924. He spent seventeen years there playing parties and clubs.

In 1941, Merriweather moved to Chicago to record for the RCA Victor subsidiary Bluebird. He recorded fourteen tracks during his first session: eight as accompanist for his new friend Tampa Red and six of his own, including the future blues standard "Worried Life Blues."

Merriweather's playing informed the work of Chicago blues keyboard masters Johnny Jones and Otis Spann. Big Maceo continued to accompany Tampa Red, as well as Big Bill Broonzy on Chicago's South Side.

After recording a series of amazing sessions as a bandleader for Bluebird in 1941–1942 and 1945 (which included his dazzling "Chicago Breakdown"), Big Maceo suffered a stroke that paralyzed his right side. Despite this disability, he persevered, returning to the studio in 1947 with Eddie Boyd on piano. Johnny Jones provided keyboard support for a 1949 Specialty Records session.

Fading health, a lifetime of heavy drinking, and his large size were all factors contributing to the 1953 heart attack that took Merriweather's short life.

He was inducted into the Blues Hall of Fame in 2002.

BIG MACEO

BIG MAYBELLE

(MABEL LOUISE SMITH)

MAIN INSTRUMENTS: Vocals, piano
BORN: Jackson, Tennessee; May 1, 1924
DIED: Cleveland, Ohio; January 23, 1972

RECOMMENDED TRACKS: "Gabbin' Blues," "Way Back Home," "My Country Man,"
"Whole Lotta Shakin' Goin' On," "St. Louis Blues," "Blues Early Early"

INTERESTING COVER: "Whole Lotta Shakin' Goin' On" (Jerry Lee Lewis)

Mabel Louise Smith's singing won her a Memphis amateur talent contest at age eight. Her subsequent gospel music foundation helped her make the switch to rhythm and blues in her teens.

In 1936, Smith joined up with Dave Clark's Memphis Band, then toured with the all-female International Sweethearts of Rhythm. She became Christine Chatman's pianist, making her recording debut with Chatman in 1944. From 1947 to 1950, Smith played with Tiny Bradshaw's Orchestra, during which she recorded three unsuccessful singles as "Mabel Smith" backed by Hot Lips Page's band.

Record producer Fred Mendelsohn rechristened her Big Maybelle, and in 1952, she signed to OKeh, Columbia's R&B subsidiary. Her first single outing, "Gabbin' Blues," shot to No. 3 on the Billboard R&B chart; Smith promptly followed with the hits "Way Back Home" and "My Country Man." In 1955 Quincy Jones produced her recording of "Whole Lotta Shakin' Goin' On," two years prior to Jerry Lee Lewis's hit version.

Big Maybelle scored again at Savoy Records with "Candy" in 1956. She continued her hard-rocking trail of Savoy hits with "Ring Dang Dilly," "That's a Pretty Good Love," and "Tell Me Who." Her blues-belting power and presence were captured in Bert Stern's 1958 Newport Jazz Festival documentary *Jazz on a Summer's Day.*

After 1959 Smith branched off into an uptown soul sound. Her 1960s repertoire ranged from gritty blues to pop ballads. The hits were sparse. Her 1967 cover of the Question Mark and the Mysterians hit "96 Tears" was her final charting single. Drugs and disease finally took their toll. Big Maybelle died far too young in a diabetic coma.

BIG MAYBELLE

LUCILLE BOGAN

(LUCILLE ANDERSON, A.K.A. BESSIE JACKSON)

MAIN INSTRUMENTS: Vocals, accordion
BORN: Amory, Mississippi; April 1, 1897
DIED: Los Angeles, California; August 10, 1948

RECOMMENDED TRACKS: "Shave 'Em Dry" (explicit version), "B.D. Woman's Blues,"
"Seaboard Blues," "Troubled Mind," "Superstitious Blues," "Black Angel Blues"

INTERESTING COVERS: "Sweet Petunia" (Blind Blake), "Tricks Ain't Walkin' No
More" (Memphis Minnie), "Gonna Leave Town" (Smokey Hogg), "Sloppy Drunk
Blues" (Leroy Carr), "Black Angel Blues" a.k.a. "Sweet Little Angel" (B.B. King)

Lucille Anderson was raised in Birmingham, Alabama, where she married rail-
wayman Nate Bogan. Her 1923 OKeh Atlanta sessions, released under the
name "Lucille Bogan," were the first time a black blues singer had made a
studio recording outside New York or Chicago. She moved to Chicago around
1925 and developed a following. In 1927 she hit with "Sweet Petunia" on
Paramount under her "Lucille Bogan" handle.

By 1930, most of her material concerned booze and sex, like "Black Angel
Blues," the original version of "Sweet Little Angel." Lucille relocated to New
York in 1933, where, as Bessie Jackson, she began her fruitful collaboration with
pianist Walter Roland. Her new moniker was not meant to hide this performer of
bawdy lyrics; instead it allowed her to sing in a different, more multilayered style.
Roland's musical ideas flowed from and enriched hers, creating a sum greater
than its parts. They recorded more than one hundred songs together before she
threw in the show biz towel in 1935. Her other accompanists included Tampa Red,
Cow Cow Davenport, Josh White, and Papa Charlie Jackson.

One of Lucille's most notorious songs is the lesbian-themed "B.D. Woman's
Blues" ("B.D." stood for "bull dyke"). Her final recordings include two takes of
"Shave 'Em Dry." The infamous, extremely explicit take is an example of frankly
sexual, after-hours-club lyrics.

Lucille managed her son's jazz group, Bogan's Birmingham Busters, then
moved to Los Angeles, where she continued to write songs. Her final composition
was the prophetically titled "Gonna Leave Town." She died from coronary sclerosis.

TRIVIA: The music critic and sexologist Ernest Borneman considered Bogan, Ma
Rainey, and Bessie Smith "the big three of the blues." Lucille's songs were once
regular repertoire for Saffire—The Uppity Blues Women, Ann Rabson, and the
Asylum Street Spankers.

LUCILLE BOGAN

EDDIE BOYD

MAIN INSTRUMENTS: Piano, vocals
BORN: Clarksdale, Mississippi; November 25, 1914
DIED: Helsinki, Finland; July 13, 1994

RECOMMENDED TRACKS: "Five Long Years," "24 Hours," "Third Degree"

INTERESTING COVERS: "Five Long Years" (Steve Marriott, Yardbirds, Eric Clapton, B.B. King, Muddy Waters, Buddy Guy), "Third Degree" (Eric Clapton)

Edward Riley Boyd moved from the Mississippi Delta to Memphis's famed Beale Street when he was twenty-two and played Roosevelt Sykes– and Leroy Carr–influenced piano as well as guitar with his band, the Dixie Rhythm Boys. In 1941 Boyd and thousands of others journeyed north to find work in the factories of Chicago.

In 1945 he backed harmonica legend John Lee "Sonny Boy" Williamson on his blues classic, "Elevator Woman." Boyd also played on Jazz Gillum's and Tampa Red's recordings. Eddie's solo debut was for RCA in 1947, where he remained through 1949.

Boyd wrote and recorded his blues standard "Five Long Years" in 1952, paying for the session himself. He then signed a Parrot contract, which was promptly sold to Chess. His rocky years at Chess produced the 1953 hits "24 Hours" and "Third Degree."

A serious auto accident in 1957 temporarily waylaid Boyd's career. His troubled relationship with Leonard Chess drove Eddie to the Bea & Baby record company in 1959, and to several lesser labels after that.

Boyd and Buddy Guy joined the American Folk Blues Festival and toured Europe in 1965. While in the U.K. Boyd took time out to record the LPs *Eddie Boyd & His Blues Band* backed by John Mayall and the Bluesbreakers and *7936 South Rhodes* backed by Peter Green's Fleetwood Mac.

Weary of American racial discrimination, Boyd moved to Belgium. He recorded with the Dutch pop group Cuby and the Blizzards and finally settled in Helsinki, Finland, in 1970. He performed often and recorded ten blues LPs there. His last blues show took place in 1984. After that, he limited himself to gospel music.

Eddie Boyd lived well in Helsinki until his death.

TRIVIA: The first of Boyd's Finnish blues LPs was titled *Praise to Helsinki*, in honor of his new home city.

EDDIE BOYD

TINY BRADSHAW

(MYRON BRADSHAW)

MAIN INSTRUMENTS: Vocals, piano, drums
BORN: Youngstown, Ohio; September 23, 1905
DIED: Cincinnati, Ohio; November 26, 1958

RECOMMENDED TRACKS: "Train Kept A-Rollin'," "Well Oh Well," "Breaking Up the House," "Soft"

INTERESTING COVERS: "Train Kept A-Rollin'" (Johnny Burnette Trio, Yardbirds as "Stroll On," Jeff Beck, Aerosmith, Motörhead)

Myron Bradshaw, who held a degree in psychology from Wilberforce University, was the vocalist for Horace Henderson's Collegians in Ohio. In 1932, Bradshaw moved to New York, where he drummed for a number of bands. Bradshaw formed his own swing orchestra in 1934, and recorded for Decca. The band struggled; they didn't record again for ten more years. By then, their swing had evolved into jump blues and R&B. They made numerous successful R&B recordings for King Records in the early 1950s. Throughout his life, Bradshaw served as a crucial and generous mentor to many important arrangers and musicians.

The talented jump-blues shouter's later career was curtailed by severe health problems, including strokes in 1954 and 1956 that left Tiny partially paralyzed. He took a few years off to recover in a Florida hospital and then slowly returned to touring. But the teenage record-buying public had moved on to rock 'n' roll. Tiny's final King single sadly sank, and though he made attempts at rock music, he had been weakened by his strokes and the physical and emotional demands of his profession. He died from a third stroke at age fifty-three.

TINY BRADSHAW

CHARLES BROWN

MAIN INSTRUMENTS: Piano, vocals

BORN: Texas City, Texas; September 13, 1922

DIED: Oakland, California; January 21, 1999

RECOMMENDED TRACKS: "Driftin' Blues," "Sunny Road," "So Long," "New Orleans Blues," "Merry Christmas, Baby," "Black Night," "Hard Times," "Trouble Blues"

INTERESTING COVER: "Driftin' Blues" (Paul Butterfield Blues Band as "Driftin' and Driftin'")

Charles Brown loved the classical piano he studied as a child. After earning a degree in chemistry from Prairie View College, he moved to Los Angeles in 1943 as one of the cool postwar Texas-style blues artists led by T-Bone Walker and Amos Milburn. L.A.'s great influx of blacks with their fresh, smooth sounds, epitomized by Nat King Cole, integrated the nightclub scene. Although musically more relaxed, adding saxophone sections to their bands demanded more formal arrangements. When Cole left to go on tour, Johnny Moore's Three Blazers, featuring Brown's mellow piano and suave, bluesy vocals, took his place.

Brown and the Blazers signed with Aladdin. His 1945 hit "Driftin' Blues" spent six months on the Billboard R&B chart, peaking at No. 2. His cool style was a major force within the influential Central Avenue club scene during that period. He inspired performers like Johnny Ace, Floyd Dixon, Percy Mayfield, and Ray Charles. Follow-up recordings for Exclusive and Modern kept the Three Blazers near the top of the R&B charts from 1946 through 1948, when Brown decided to go solo.

Even bigger on his own, Brown hit the R&B Top 10 at least ten times from 1949 to 1952 with his mournful, spare groove, including "Trouble Blues," which reached No. 1. Brown's relaxed sound failed to surmount rock's increasingly rougher approach, however. Except for "Please Come Home for Christmas," a perennial million seller, Charles Brown's star faded. During the 1960s he recorded two LPs. His 1980s shows at the New York club Tramps resulted in him signing with Blue Side Records. Though the label went under, its distribution for Brown's 1986 album *One More for the Road* was picked up by Alligator. After that LP hit, Bonnie Raitt brought him on tour with her as her opener.

Brown's recording career was reestablished with a series of Bullseye Blues albums and a Verve disc. He finally began to rise to the prominence he deserved as a genuine R&B groundbreaker, achieving his greatest recording and performing success since the 1950s and receiving several Grammy nominations. The eternally suave musician put out *So Goes Love* in 1998, shortly before dying of congestive heart failure.

CHARLES BROWN

CLARENCE "GATEMOUTH" BROWN

MAIN INSTRUMENTS: Vocals, guitar, fiddle,
mandolin, viola, harmonica, drums
BORN: Vinton, Louisiana; April 18, 1924
DIED: Orange, Texas; September 10, 2005

RECOMMENDED TRACKS: "My Time Is Expensive," "Boogie Uproar," "Okie Dokie
Stomp," "She Walked Right In," "Dirty Work at the Crossroad"

Clarence Brown's stage name came from a high school teacher in Texas who proclaimed he had a "voice like a gate."

Originally a drummer, he became a superb guitarist. His big break came in 1947 during a concert at Don Robey's Bronze Peacock nightclub in Houston. When headliner T-Bone Walker fell ill, Brown took the stage and played a rousing "Gatemouth Boogie." In 1949 Robey created his own Peacock label just to showcase the searing guitar of Brown, who remained with the label through 1960.

Brown's sole chart success was the 1949 double-sided hit "Mary Is Fine"/"My Time Is Expensive." His groundbreaking music, though, is a major part of Texas's rich postwar blues legacy that strongly influenced Houston guitarists like Albert Collins and Johnny "Guitar" Watson.

Brown's career lagged in the 1960s, except for a brief 1966 run as house bandleader for *The !!!! Beat*, an innovative syndicated R&B TV show. By the late 1960s, he had left the music biz and became a New Mexico deputy sheriff.

Clarence Brown benefited from the 1970s European blues resurgence, often playing 300 shows a year. Gatemouth served as an official American music ambassador on several U.S. State Department–sponsored tours. Mastering many instruments, Gate completely rebuilt his career, playing country, jazz, and calypso. After recording with the pianist Professor Longhair in 1974, Gate moved to New Orleans. He cut *Makin' Music*, a 1979 duet LP, with his pal Roy Clark, and appeared frequently on TV's *Hee Haw*. A slew of acclaimed CDs Brown recorded up through the 2000s revealed an unclassifiable American original. His *Alright Again!* won the 1982 Grammy for Best Traditional Blues Album.

Brown toured the world until 2004, when, already suffering from emphysema and heart disease, he was diagnosed with lung cancer. Hurricane Katrina forced Brown to relocate to Orange, Texas, where he died in his niece's apartment.

TRIVIA: Frank Zappa named Clarence Brown as his all-time favorite guitarist.

CLARENCE "GATEMOUTH" BROWN

ROY BROWN

MAIN INSTRUMENT: Vocals
BORN: New Orleans, Louisiana; September 10, 1925
DIED: Pacoima, California; May 25, 1981

RECOMMENDED TRACKS: "Good Rockin' Tonight," "Hard Luck Blues," "Miss Fanny Brown," "Ain't No Rockin' No More," "Let the Four Winds Blow"

INTERESTING COVERS: "Good Rockin' Tonight" (Wynonie Harris, Elvis Presley, Ricky Nelson, Montrose), "Let the Four Winds Blow" (Fats Domino)

Roy James Brown was raised by his mother, an accomplished singer and church organist, in Eunice, Louisiana; Houston, Texas; and Los Angeles, where he won a 1945 singing contest covering "There's No You" by Bing Crosby, his favorite singer. In 1946 Brown moved to Galveston, Texas, where he mostly performed current hits. Classified 4-F for his flat feet during WWII, Brown snagged a nine-month Shreveport, Louisiana, club gig as a pop ballads singer (hired because he was "a Negro who sounds white"). He began adding blues numbers to his repertoire.

Roy moved to New Orleans in 1947, where a blues pianist heard his composition "Good Rockin' Tonight" (written for and originally rejected by Wynonie Harris) and convinced him to sing it over the phone to DeLuxe Records' president at 4 A.M. Brown was signed immediately. "Good Rockin' Tonight" hit No. 13 on the Billboard R&B chart, and Brown became the king of R&B, charting 15 hits from 1948 to 1951; "Hard Luck Blues" (1950) was his biggest seller. His sales then crashed. He sued King Records in 1952 over a royalty dispute and, amazingly, won. This may have led to Brown's being blacklisted. His misfortunes were compounded by prison time for tax evasion.

Brown briefly scored again with "Let the Four Winds Blow," cowritten with Fats Domino and recorded for Imperial in 1957, and later becoming a hit for Fats. Roy worked various nonmusical jobs and recorded some in the 1960s, then sold the rights to "Good Rockin' Tonight" and worked as an encyclopedia salesman.

After a long dry spell, Brown closed the Johnny Otis set at the 1970 Monterey Jazz Festival to great acclaim, then he recorded "Love for Sale," a Mercury hit. Brown died of a heart attack a few weeks after he headlined the 1981 New Orleans Jazz and Heritage Festival. The Reverend Johnny Otis conducted the funeral.

Roy Brown was the first to blend gospel's call-and-response with the blues.

TRIVIA: When Brown was in financial trouble, he approached Elvis Presley for help. Elvis immediately found a piece of plain brown paper and wrote Roy a check.

ROY BROWN

GUS CANNON

(A.K.A. BANJO JOE)

MAIN INSTRUMENTS: Banjo, jug, vocals, fiddle
BORN: Red Banks, Mississippi; September 12, 1883 (or 1874)
DIED: Memphis, Tennessee; October 15, 1979

RECOMMENDED TRACKS: "Minglewood Blues," "Pig Ankle Strut," "Wolf River Blues,"
"Viola Lee Blues," "White House Station," "Walk Right In"

INTERESTING COVERS: "Minglewood Blues" (Grateful Dead), "Viola Lee Blues"
(Grateful Dead), "Walk Right In" (Rooftop Singers, Dr. Hook and the Medicine Show)

Plantation-born Gus Cannon (his birth year is a subject of dispute) moved to Clarksdale, Mississippi, at the age of twelve. He constructed his first banjo from a frying pan and raccoon skin. Guitarist Alex Lee taught Cannon his first folk blues, and showed him how to use a pocketknife to play slide guitar.

At fifteen, Gus ran away from home, performing for years at Mississippi Delta sawmills, levee camps, and railroad camps. Around 1907, Cannon left for Memphis. He played in Jim Guffin's jug band and then met harmonica ace Noah Lewis, who introduced him to guitarist Ashley Thompson. The trio played dances and parties. In 1914, Cannon took off to work in medicine shows.

As "Banjo Gus," Cannon's recording career commenced with solo sessions for Paramount in 1927. Inspired by the success of the local Memphis Jug Band, Gus quickly formed the epitome of jugband music, Cannon's Jug Stompers, featuring Lewis and Thompson and, later, singer Hosea Woods. Despite making their last records in 1930, Cannon's Jug Stompers remained one of Memphis's most popular jug bands through the rest of the decade. Gus continued to record on the side, both solo and as Banjo Joe with Blind Blake.

By 1940, Cannon had virtually retired. He did yard work, sharecropped, and dug ditches. He resumed recording, albeit sporadically, for Folkways in 1956. Gus worked with Furry Lewis and Bukka White during the 1960s blues revival. After Cannon's song "Walk Right In" became a hit for the Rooftop Singers, he recorded a Stax LP with Will Shade, the former leader of the Memphis Jug Band. Gus still played the odd show, at times from a wheelchair, until just before his death.

An extraordinary musician who could play banjo and jug simultaneously, Gus Cannon was the human musical link between the dawn of the blues and earlier minstrel and folk music forms.

TRIVIA: Gus made the first recording ever of slide banjo. He can be seen in the late-night wedding scene in the 1929 King Vidor film *Hallelujah!*.

GUS CANNON

IDA COX

(IDA PRATHER, A.K.A. KATE LEWIS, VELMA BRADLEY, JULIA POWERS, JANE SMITH)

MAIN INSTRUMENT: Vocals
BORN: Tocoa, Georgia; February 25, 1896
DIED: Knoxville, Tennessee; November 10, 1967

RECOMMENDED TRACKS: "Wild Women Don't Have the Blues," "Death Letter Blues"

NOT A COVER: "Four Day Creep," as performed by the English rock group Humble Pie, although credited to Ida Cox, is not the same as her "'Fore Day Creep." Ida's title refers to the clandestine visit one pays to or receives from a lover (be)fore day(break).

I da Prather grew up in Cedartown, Georgia, singing in the African Methodist church choir and, by age fourteen, in theaters. She ran away from home to tour the South with minstrel, vaudeville, and tent shows as a singer and comedian, often appearing in blackface well into the 1910s. She married fellow minstrel performer Adler Cox.

By 1920, Ida Cox had become a vaudeville headliner in Atlanta, Georgia, and she sang with jazz greats Jelly Roll Morton and King Oliver in Chicago.

The demand for "race music" became apparent after the breakthrough success of Mamie Smith's 1920 recording of "Crazy Blues," sparking the classic female blues era, epitomized by 1920s singers like Bessie Smith and Ma Rainey. In 1923, Ida signed with Paramount, where she stayed for six years, recording seventy-eight songs for them and headlining touring companies billed as the Sepia Mae West or the Uncrowned Queen of Blues. She also managed two successive vaudeville troupes, Ida Cox and Her Raisin' Cain Company and then Darktown Scandals. She increased her recorded output during the 1920s by using pseudonyms to maneuver around exclusivity clauses in her Paramount contract.

In 1934 Ida and Bessie Smith appeared in the Apollo Theater revue *Fan Waves*. Despite not recording during most of the 1930s, Cox still worked. In 1939 she sang at Café Society in New York and appeared in John Hammond's *From Spirituals to Swing* Carnegie Hall concert. This briefly revitalized her recording career, and she sessioned with jazz artists Lionel Hampton, Fletcher Henderson, and Hot Lips Page. Cox signed with Vocalion Records and then OKeh Records.

Ida Cox toured with a number of shows until suffering a stroke on stage in 1944. She left show business and moved to Knoxville, Tennessee, to live with her daughter. She was coaxed out of retirement in 1961 for one final LP, *Blues for Rampart Street*, accompanied by Coleman Hawkins. She died of cancer.

ARTHUR "BIG BOY" CRUDUP

(A.K.A. ELMER JAMES, PERCY LEE CRUDUP)

MAIN INSTRUMENTS: Vocals, guitar
BORN: Forest, Mississippi; August 5, 1905
DIED: Nassawadox, Virginia; March 28, 1974

RECOMMENDED TRACKS: "That's All Right," "My Baby Left Me," "So Glad You're Mine," "Rock Me Mama," "Ethel Mae," "Mean Old 'Frisco Blues"

INTERESTING COVERS: "That's All Right," "My Baby Left Me," "So Glad You're Mine" (all by Elvis Presley)

n his youth, Arthur Crudup labored as a migrant worker all over the South and Midwest. He sang gospel, then switched to the blues. After visiting Chicago with the Harmonizing Four in 1939, Crudup remained there, trying to eke out a living as a street singer.

In 1941, producer Lester Melrose discovered Arthur living in a packing crate underneath an elevated train track. He hired Crudup to play a party that night at Tampa Red's house, which was attended by Melrose's clients Big Bill Broonzy, Lonnie Johnson, and Lil Green. Arthur's performance got him an RCA/Bluebird record deal. He rocked the R&B charts with a string of hits, although his original recording of "That's All Right" wasn't a national hit. Around 1948 Crudup toured the country with Sonny Boy Williamson II and Elmore James. He stayed with RCA until 1954 (in the early 1950s he recorded for Ace, Trumpet, and Checker under pseudonyms), when his battles over royalty payments (Elvis had massively successful hit covers of Crudup's songs for RCA) turned him against the company and he stopped recording.

Crudup returned to Mississippi, and went into bootlegging. He resurfaced seven years later with an album mostly consisting of remakes of his own hits. In 1965, Delmark Records' boss tracked down the musician in Virginia on a tip from Big Joe Williams. Crudup's Delmark recordings finally gave Arthur a chance to earn some good dough, allowing him to play various blues and folk festivals to enthusiastic audiences.

In the mid-1960s, Crudup returned to bootlegging and farmwork. In the early 1970s, two local Virginia activists failed in their attempt to help him gain his lost royalties. Arthur's last public shows were with Bonnie Raitt. He died of a heart attack as a result of complications from heart disease and diabetes.

TRIVIA: Arthur did not learn guitar until he was thirty years old. Disgruntled because of his lost royalties, he referred to admirer Elvis Presley as "Elvin Preston."

COW COW DAVENPORT

(CHARLES EDWARD DAVENPORT)

MAIN INSTRUMENTS: Piano, vocals, organ
BORN: Anniston, Alabama; April 23, 1894
DIED: Cleveland, Ohio; December 3, 1955

RECOMMENDED TRACKS: "Cow Cow Blues," "Chimin' the Blues," "State Street Jive," "Shadow Blues" (with Ivy Smith), "Mama Don't Allow No Easy Riders"

INTERESTING COVER: "Cow Cow Blues" (Ella Mae Morse)

Charles Davenport's family fiercely opposed his musical ambitions. They shipped him off to a theological seminary, from which he was promptly expelled for playing that frisky ragtime music.

Davenport's career began in the 1920s when he joined a traveling medicine show. On the Theater Owners Booking Association circuit vaudeville tours in the 1920s and early '30s, he usually supported vocalists Dora Carr and Ivy (or Iva) Smith. Davenport and Smith put together a fairly unsuccessful touring revue. He was regularly jailed for using their tour bus as loan collateral. By the time he was finally freed, arthritis had cost him the use of his right arm.

He recorded the song that gave him his stage name, the blues-ragtime hybrid "Cow Cow Blues," in 1925. Although Ray Charles is credited as "adapting" "Pine Top's Boogie Woogie" for his song "Mess Around" (with authorship credited to "A. Nugetre," a.k.a. Atlantic Records chief Ahmet Ertegun), the opening piano riff to "Mess Around" is derived from "Cow Cow Blues." The dance known as "The Mess Around" is mentioned in Cow Cow's song "Mooch Piddle."

Cow Cow claimed he wrote Washboard Sam's hit "Mama Don't Allow It" and Louis Armstrong's "I'll Be Glad When You're Dead, You Rascal You," selling the royalty rights and composer credits. Cow Cow performed with Tampa Red and recorded for several labels from 1929 through 1946; after 1938, because of his physical limitations, Sam Price often filled in on piano. Davenport was also a versatile composer and talent scout for Vocalion.

Cow Cow suffered a stroke in the early 1930s and lost fine movement in his fingers. In 1938 jazz pianist Art Hodes discovered him washing dishes. Hodes assisted Davenport in securing him new recording contracts. Eventually, the poverty-stricken musician died from hardening of the arteries.

TRIVIA: The 1943 hit from Abbott and Costello's movie *Ride 'Em Cowboy*, "Cow-Cow Boogie (Cuma-Ti-Yi-Yi-Ay)," was probably named in honor of Davenport.

COW COW DAVENPORT

WALTER DAVIS

(A.K.A. HOOKER JOE)

MAIN INSTRUMENTS: Vocals, piano
BORN: Grenada, Mississippi; March 1, 1912
DIED: St. Louis, Missouri (likely); October 22, 1963

RECOMMENDED TRACKS: "I Think You Need a Shot," "Angel Child," "M & O Blues," "Come Back Baby," "You Are the One I Love," "Sunnyland Blues," "Blue Blues"

INTERESTING COVERS: "I Think You Need a Shot" (Stone the Crows as "Penicillin Blues"), "M & O Blues" (Memphis Slim), "Angel Child" (Robert Lockwood Jr.), "Come Back Baby" (Ray Charles, Bert Jansch, Love Sculpture, Lowell Fulson)

Walter Davis was born on a farm. He took off from home at about age thirteen, ending up in St. Louis, Missouri. His robust piano style was strongly influenced by Leroy Carr, although Davis was much better known for his rich, somberly expressive vocals than for his mastery of the keyboard. Carr also influenced Walter's songwriting, as reflected in the bawdy content of Davis's lyrics to "I Think You Need a Shot."

Roosevelt Sykes supported Walter on his first recordings, made from 1930 to 1933, until Davis had improved and polished his chops and self-assurance. He made nearly 180 recordings between 1930 and 1952, several of which were covered by other singers. From the late 1920s through the early 1950s, Davis played Southern and lower Midwestern clubs, usually with pals Henry Townsend and Peetie Wheatstraw. Walter's later recordings are generally regarded as his best.

His success stalled when he began to suffer from health issues. He stopped performing around 1953. After a stroke, he put down roots in St. Louis, working as a hotel night clerk and preacher. The exact place of his death is uncertain, though it's most likely St. Louis. It's rumored he was still sermonizing right up until he passed.

WALTER DAVIS

BO DIDDLEY

(ELLAS OTHA BATES, ELLAS MCDANIEL)

MAIN INSTRUMENTS: Guitar, vocals
BORN: McComb, Mississippi; December 30, 1928
DIED: Archer, Florida; June 2, 2008

RECOMMENDED TRACKS: "Bo Diddley," "I'm a Man," "Diddley Daddy," "Pretty Thing," "Diddy Wah Diddy," "Who Do You Love?," "Mona (I Need You Baby)," "Road Runner," "I Can Tell," "You Can't Judge a Book by Its Cover"

INTERESTING COVERS: "I'm a Man" (Yardbirds), "Diddley Daddy" (Chris Isaak), "Pretty Thing" (Pretty Things), "Bring It to Jerome" (Manfred Mann), "Who Do You Love?" (Quicksilver Messenger Service), "Mona (I Need You Baby)" (Rolling Stones), "I Can Tell" (John Hammond), "Love Is Strange" (Mickey & Sylvia)

INTERESTING TRIBUTE: "The Story of Bo Diddley" (Animals)

Bo was adopted and raised by his mother's cousin, Gussie McDaniel. In 1934, his family moved to Chicago's South Side. He studied trombone and violin, excelling at the latter (his violin playing is featured in the song "The Clock Strikes Twelve"), but became fascinated by the guitar.

Inspired by John Lee Hooker, Bo played street corners with friends, including maraca man Jerome Green, in a band called the Hipsters (a.k.a. the Langley Avenue Jive Cats). During 1943 and 1944, he played for street tips in a band with Earl Hooker, and by 1951 he had a regular gig on Chicago's South Side. In 1954 he recorded demos of "Bo Diddley" and "I'm a Man," then rerecorded them for Chess after they were rejected by Vee-Jay. "Bo Diddley" became a No. 1 R&B hit in 1955, and from 1958 through 1963 Checker released eleven Bo Diddley LPs and a handful more during the rest of the 1960s.

Bo Diddley was a key link between blues and rock 'n' roll. His "Bo Diddley beat" resembled the "shave and a haircut" rhythm he discovered while trying to play Gene Autry's "(I've Got Spurs That) Jingle, Jangle, Jingle." Bo's wisecracking lyrics displayed a comically endearing jive and sass.

From 1971 to 1978 Bo continued touring while maintaining a residence in Los Lunas, New Mexico, where he served for two and a half years as a deputy sheriff. He made Archer, Florida, his home base for the last thirteen years of his life. Bo died from heart failure not long after suffering a stroke and a heart attack.

TRIVIA: In 1955, he was banned from *The Ed Sullivan Show* for life after singing "Bo Diddley" live instead of "Sixteen Tons" as promised.

BO DIDDLEY

WILLIE DIXON

MAIN INSTRUMENTS: Bass, vocals, guitar
BORN: Vicksburg, Mississippi; July 1, 1915
DIED: Burbank, California; January 29, 1992

RECOMMENDED TRACKS: Chess's *Willie Dixon* box set is a comprehensive introduction to the man's songwriting skills.

INTERESTING COVERS: "Back Door Man" (Doors), "I Ain't Superstitious" (Jeff Beck Group), "I Can't Quit You Baby" (Led Zeppelin), "I Just Want to Make Love to You" (Foghat), "I'm Ready" (Humble Pie), "Little Red Rooster" (Rolling Stones), "Seventh Son" (Johnny Rivers), "Spoonful" (Cream, Paul Butterfield Blues Band), "Wang Dang Doodle" (Love Sculpture), "You Need Love" (Small Faces, Led Zeppelin as "Whole Lotta Love"), "You Shook Me" (Jeff Beck Group, Led Zeppelin), "My Babe" (Tom Jones), "You Can't Judge a Book by Its Cover" (Rolling Stones), "Bring It On Home" (Led Zeppelin)

At age seven, William James Dixon first heard the blues being played by Little Brother Montgomery. He learned to sing harmonies from carpenter Leo Phelps and sang bass in Leo's Union Jubilee Singers. Dixon began turning his poems into songs and selling them to local bands. The 1937 Illinois State Golden Gloves Heavyweight Champion, he met his harmonizing partner, Leonard "Baby Doo" Caston, at the gym. Baby Doo created Willie's first bass from a tin can and a string. Moving up to the real instrument, Dixon began playing in Chicago and cofounded the Bluebird blues-jazz harmony group the Five Breezes. After ten months in prison as a conscientious objector, Willie formed two groups with Baby Doo: the Four Jumps of Jive and the Big Three Trio.

Dixon signed to Chess Records as a recording artist, but was more involved as a full-time producer, talent scout, session musician, and staff songwriter—all for just one hundred bucks a week! His time at Chess ended after Leonard Chess's death in 1969. Dixon questioned his contract with Chess's publishing arm, Arc Music. He had seen little money from his songs, despite hit British versions. Arc sued Led Zeppelin over "Bring It On Home" and won, but Dixon never saw any settlement money until he sued Arc. He also sued Zeppelin over "Whole Lotta Love" (a retitled and instrumentally rearranged version of Dixon's "You Need Love"). Both cases resulted in generous out-of-court settlements.

Willie was the most vital composer of what is now considered the Great American Songbook of the Blues. His songs are the virtual foundation of the British blues movement. The initial classic performances of his songs were by the artists he produced in Chicago: Muddy Waters, Howlin' Wolf, Little Walter, Bo Diddley, Koko Taylor, Sonny Boy Williamson, Willie Mabon, and Little Milton.

WILLIE DIXON

"GEORGIA TOM" DORSEY

(THOMAS ANDREW DORSEY)

MAIN INSTRUMENT: Piano
BORN: Villa Rica, Georgia; July 1, 1899
DIED: Chicago, Illinois; January 23, 1993

RECOMMENDED TRACKS: "It's Tight Like That," "All Alone Blues," "Maybe It's the Blues," "Grievin' Me Blues," "Broke Man's Blues," "Pig Meat Blues"

INTERESTING COVER: "It's Tight Like That" (Clara Smith)

Tom Dorsey's minister father and piano teacher mother encouraged him musically even when he was a toddler. He loved all kinds of music, but blues and ragtime were his teen passions. He played rent parties as Barrelhouse Tom, Texas Tommy, and, finally, Georgia Tom.

In 1918, Dorsey studied music in Chicago and became a Paramount agent, then formed the Wildcats Jazz Band to back Ma Rainey in 1924. Gigs paid poorly, so Tom turned to songwriting. One of the songs he wrote with Tampa Red, "It's Tight Like That," sold seven million copies. Dorsey is ultimately credited with writing more than four hundred blues and jazz songs, many with incredibly poetic lyrics.

Georgia Tom began recording gospel music alongside blues in the mid-1920s. By 1932, as Chicago's Pilgrim Baptist Church's music director, he became more closely involved with church music. He started one of the nation's first gospel choirs and was a founder and the first president of the National Convention of Gospel Choirs and Choruses. Dissatisfied with the treatment of black gospel songwriters by white music publishers, Tom founded Dorsey House of Music, the first publishing firm solely devoted to the compositions of black gospel artists. He also promoted the careers of singers like Mahalia Jackson.

Dorsey's first wife, Nettie, had been Ma Rainey's wardrobe mistress. In 1932 she perished in childbirth, followed two days later by their baby son. From the depths of Tom's great anguish emerged one of the most famous gospel songs of all time, "Take My Hand, Precious Lord."

TRIVIA: Known as the father of gospel music, Dorsey was so closely linked with the field that at one time, gospel songs were known as "dorseys." The Nashville Songwriters Hall of Fame voted to include Tom, the first African American to earn that honor. The Gospel Music Association also made Dorsey the first inductee in their Living Hall of Fame. Dr. Martin Luther King Jr. and President Lyndon B. Johnson both requested that "Take My Hand, Precious Lord" be sung at their funerals.

"GEORGIATOM" DORSEY

CHAMPION JACK DUPREE

(WILLIAM THOMAS DUPREE)

MAIN INSTRUMENTS: Piano, vocals
BORN: New Orleans area (?); July 4, 10, or 23 in 1908, 1909, or 1910
DIED: Hannover, Germany; January 21, 1992

RECOMMENDED TRACKS: "Shim Sham Shimmy," "Mail Order Woman," "Junker's Blues," "Nasty Boogie," "TB Blues," "Angola Blues," "Dupree Shake Dance"

INTERESTING COVER: "Junker's Blues" (Fats Domino as "The Fat Man")

At age two, William Dupree was left an orphan (he claimed that his parents perished in either a blaze ignited by the Ku Klux Klan or an accidental fire) and sent to New Orleans's Colored Waif's Home for Boys, Louis Armstrong's alma mater. Dupree was mentored by pianists Tuts Washington and Willie "Drive 'Em Down" Hall, whom he called his father and from whom he learned "Junker's Blues." After playing barrelhouses and other gin joints, Dupree left New Orleans in 1930 for Chicago, where he performed with Georgia Tom. He worked as a cook in Indianapolis, Indiana, where he encountered Leroy Carr and Scrapper Blackwell. While in Detroit, Joe Louis urged Jack to box professionally. By 1935, Dupree had more than one hundred bouts under his belt and was a multiple Golden Gloves champion, earning him his nickname.

Champion Jack returned to Chicago, joining Big Bill Broonzy and Tampa Red. In 1940, Dupree made his OKeh recording debut with "Warehouse Man Blues" and "Black Woman Swing." A WWII Navy cook, he ended up as a Japanese prisoner of war for two years. In 1949, his driving "Junker's Blues" got retooled as Fats Domino's debut, "The Fat Man." Dupree finally gave up boxing and became a New York recording artist for five different companies. He got around his contracts' exclusivity clauses by recording as Brother Blues, Lightnin' Jr., and Meat Head Johnson.

Despite fine King Records work from 1953 to 1955, his only charter was "Walking the Blues." Dupree recorded his barrelhouse masterpiece, *Blues from the Gutter*, for Atlantic in 1958.

The following year, Dupree became one of the first bluesmen to leave the United States for the less racist Europe. He lived in various countries, frequently recording for Storyville, British Decca (with John Mayall and Eric Clapton), and many others. He played the 1990 Jazz and Heritage Festival and cut *Back Home in New Orleans* and two more LPs of new material just prior to his death from cancer.

CHAMPION JACK DUPREE

BLIND BOY FULLER

(FULTON ALLEN)

MAIN INSTRUMENTS: Guitar, vocals
BORN: Wadesboro, North Carolina; July 10, 1907
DIED: Durham, North Carolina; February 13, 1941

RECOMMENDED TRACKS: "Rag, Mama, Rag," "Truckin' My Blues Away," "Get Your Yas Yas Out," "Step It Up and Go," "Mamie," "Rattlesnakin' Daddy"

One of ten children, Fulton Allen learned guitar, field hollers, country rags, blues, and traditional songs from older singers. In his midteens he began to lose his eyesight from ulcers behind his eyes caused by snowblindness or by chemicals thrown in his face by an ex-girlfriend. By 1928 Fulton was completely blind. Still, he became a skilled guitarist by listening to the records of Blind Blake and studying the live performances of Gary Davis. Allen performed on the streets and at parties in Winston-Salem, North Carolina, and Danville, Virginia, then graduated to playing the more lucrative tobacco warehouse district in Durham, North Carolina. His following grew to include harp player Sonny Terry.

Fulton recorded more than 120 songs over a five-year span. He was the most popular Piedmont blues artist (a ragtime-influenced group of pickers that included Blind Blake, Josh White, and Buddy Moss). His singing style was bold, raw, and unsentimentally honest. Allen worked with Reverend Gary Davis, and in 1935 he got a New York session with the American Recording Company (ARC). They rechristened Allen "Blind Boy Fuller" and Washington "Bull City Red."

In 1936 Fuller made ten solo recordings. After doing more for Decca, he returned to ARC and recorded with Sonny Terry. In 1938, the reputedly hotheaded Fuller shot his wife in the leg. He was replaced by Terry when his imprisonment caused him to miss performing at John Hammond's career-altering *From Spirituals to Swing* concerts at Carnegie Hall. After his release, Fuller's final recording sessions took place in New York in 1940. Despite his vast recorded output, he spent most of his career playing street corners and house parties.

Like Robert Johnson, Fuller lived fast and died young, undergoing surgery for a blocked bladder (perhaps due to excessive drinking) in 1940. He then died of widespread abscesses caused by kidney failure and several lower abdominal infections.

TRIVIA: The Rolling Stones' *Get Yer Ya-Ya's Out!* LP was named after Fuller's "Get Your Yas Yas Out." R. Crumb's phrase "Keep on truckin'" first appeared in the lyrics to Blind Boy's "Truckin' My Blues Away."

BLIND BOY FULLER

JESSE FULLER

(A.K.A. LONE CAT)

MAIN INSTRUMENTS: Vocals, one-man band (including the fotdella)
BORN: Jonesboro, Georgia; March 12, 1896
DIED: Oakland, California; January 29, 1976

RECOMMENDED TRACKS: "San Francisco Bay Blues," "Beat It On Down the Line"

INTERESTING COVERS: "San Francisco Bay Blues" (Janis Joplin, Eric Clapton, Paul McCartney), "The Monkey and the Engineer" (Grateful Dead), "You're No Good" (Bob Dylan)

Mistreated by cruel foster parents, the youthful Jesse Fuller grazed cows, shined shoes, and worked in a barrel factory, a broom factory, a rock quarry, and for a railroad and streetcar company. He even peddled hand-carved wooden snakes.

Fuller joined a circus and left Georgia in 1920. He hoboed across the United States, eventually settling in Los Angeles, where he worked as a film extra, appearing in *The Thief of Bagdad*, among other movies. He moved to Oakland, then labored as a shipyard welder during WWII.

At the age of fifty-five, Fuller decided to become a professional musician. He had learned but a little guitar as a child, yet he soon amassed a sizable song repertoire: country blues, work songs, ballads, and spirituals. When it became difficult to find other musicians with whom to work, he became a one-man band.

Fuller's arsenal of instruments included a twelve-string guitar, harmonica, kazoo, hi-hat, and fotdella. His own invention, the fotdella was a large upright wooden box shaped like the top of a double bass. Six bass strings, attached to a short neck, stretched over the body, each a different note when tuned. Jesse played them with six foot pedals connected to padded hammers. The six available notes enabled him to play bass in several keys. His wife called the contraption a "foot-diller" (a "killer-diller" instrument played with a foot), and the name sprang from that.

After beginning in Bay Area clubs and bars, Jesse Fuller made appearances on San Francisco and Los Angeles television stations. His career took off in 1954 when he wrote "San Francisco Bay Blues," leading to his successful first LP, *Folk Blues: Working on the Railroad with Jesse Fuller* on the Good Time Jazz record label in 1955. He cut records for other labels and became a prominent figure in the 1960s blues revival. He toured throughout America and Europe, performing at 1960s and '70s blues and folk festivals between a plethora of coffeehouses. Fuller continued to play and record until his death from heart disease.

JESSE FULLER

LOWELL FULSON

(A.K.A. LOWELL FULSOM, LOWELL FULLSOM)

MAIN INSTRUMENTS: Guitar, vocals
BORN: Tulsa, Oklahoma; March 31, 1921
DIED: Long Beach, California; March 6, 1999

RECOMMENDED TRACKS: "Reconsider Baby," "Three O'Clock Blues," "Every Day I Have the Blues," "Tramp," "Blue Shadows," "Low Society Blues," "Loving You"

INTERESTING COVERS: "Reconsider Baby" (Chicken Shack, Eric Clapton, Elvis Presley, Sir Douglas Quintet), "Tramp" (Otis Redding and Carla Thomas, Julie Driscoll and the Brian Auger Trinity), "Three O'Clock Blues" (B.B. King), "Sinner's Prayer" (Ray Charles)

Sources claim Fulson was born on a Choctaw reservation (Fulson boasted of both Cherokee and Choctaw ancestry), where he was exposed to local blues and Bob Wills's western swing. In 1940, he moved to Ada, Oklahoma. He briefly joined Alger "Texas" Alexander and toured the state of Texas with veteran bluesmen. The U.S. Navy drafted him in 1943. After the war ended, he spent a few months back in Oklahoma, then moved to Oakland, California, where he made his first recordings, eventually becoming the most significant West Coast bluesman of the 1940s and '50s next to T-Bone Walker.

The big-voiced guitarist and songwriter cut records for small labels and had a 1948 hit with "Three O'Clock Blues" on Down Town Records. Swing Time signed Fulson that year. Lowell had a string of hits for them in the early 1950s, including "Every Day I Have the Blues" (an adaptation of Memphis Slim's "Nobody Loves Me"). He toured heavily with a band that briefly included Ray Charles.

Fulson signed with Checker in 1954. His first Checker single, the blues classic "Reconsider Baby," was a massive hit. With the exception of "Loving You," his subsequent singles on that label failed to chart. He left Checker in 1962 and joined L.A.'s Kent Records, where "Black Nights" (1965) became his first hit in more than ten years. "Tramp" went even higher, reestablishing him as an R&B star. After some modest Kent hits, he signed with Jewel. From the 1970s to the '90s, he recorded solid LPs for Bullseye. Health issues forced him to retire in 1997. He passed away a few weeks before his seventy-eighth birthday.

TRIVIA: For contractual reasons, Fulson also recorded as Lowell Fullsom and Lowell Fulsom. His 1970 cover of the Beatles' "Why Don't We Do It in the Road?" appeared on the 2007 *American Gangster* soundtrack. In the 2004 film on Ray Charles's life, *Ray*, Fulson was portrayed by blues musician Chris Thomas King.

LOWELL FULSON

JAZZ GILLUM

(WILLIAM MCKINLEY GILLUM)

MAIN INSTRUMENTS: Harmonica, vocals
BORN: Indianola, Mississippi; September 11, 1904
DIED: Chicago, Illinois; March 29, 1966

RECOMMENDED TRACKS: "Key to the Highway," "Reefer Headed Woman," "Look on Yonder Wall"

INTERESTING COVERS: "Key to the Highway" (Little Walter, Steve Miller Band, Derek and the Dominos, the Band, Freddie King), "Look on Yonder Wall" (Elmore James, Steve Miller Band, Arthur "Big Boy" Crudup, Freddie King)

At age seven, Jazz Gillum and his brothers fled their harsh deacon uncle's home to live with relatives in Charleston, Mississippi, where he spent the next twelve years playing harmonica on street corners for tips while also working as a field hand and in a drugstore. He moved to Chicago in 1923 and connected with guitarist Big Bill Broonzy. The duo worked the clubs. By 1934, Gillum had recorded for both the American Recording Company and Bluebird Records. With Broonzy featured on guitar, Jazz Gillum was the first to record "Key to the Highway" as an eight-bar blues (it was first recorded by Charlie Segar, but with a different melody and arrangement). Broonzy's rearranged cover, recorded just months later, became the standard version of this blues classic.

Aside from Sonny Boy Williamson, no harmonica player was more popular or in demand as a session man during the 1930s than Gillum. His high, reedy sound perfectly complemented Bluebird's hokum (songs with humorous sexual innuendos) records, in both his work as a solo artist and as a sideman in the Bluebird house band in the 1930s and '40s. Teenage jazz guitarist George Barnes was featured on the 1938 Gillum session that produced "Reefer Headed Woman" and other blues numbers—among the very first electric guitar blues recordings.

Gillum served in the U.S. Army from 1942 to 1945. He created "Look on Yonder Wall" in 1946 with Big Maceo; it later became an Elmore James hit. Jazz Gillum's recording career dried up after Bluebird went under in the late 1940s. His last sessions were in 1961 with Memphis Slim. In 1966 Gillum was shot in the head during a street argument, and died before he reached Garfield Park Hospital.

TRIVIA: Gillum's daughter, Ardella Williams, is a blues singer in Chicago.

JAZZ GILLUM

GUITAR SLIM

(EDDIE JONES)

MAIN INSTRUMENTS: Guitar, vocals
BORN: Greenwood, Mississippi; December 10, 1926
DIED: New York, New York; February 7, 1959

RECOMMENDED TRACKS: "The Things That I Used to Do," "Well I Done Got Over It," "It Hurts to Love Someone," "Down Through the Years," "Feelin' Sad," "The Story of My Life," "Sufferin' Mind," "Quicksand," "If I Should Lose You"

INTERESTING COVERS: "The Things That I Used to Do" (Stevie Ray Vaughan), "Feelin' Sad" (Ray Charles)

As a teenager Eddie Jones worked in the cotton fields, and hung out at the local juke joints in his free time. By often filling in as a singer and dancer, he earned the nickname "Limber Leg."

His guitar work was especially influenced by Clarence "Gatemouth" Brown and T-Bone Walker. Around 1950 he became "Guitar Slim," known for his flamboyant stage show. He dyed his hair to match his bright-colored suits, playing as he strolled through his audiences with a 350-foot cord connecting his amplifier and guitar. He would perform mounted on his assistant's shoulders, or take his guitar outside the club and bring traffic to a stop. He distorted his guitar more than a decade before rock guitarists did so. His gospel-enriched vocals made him easily identifiable.

Slim joined up with Muddy Waters in Los Angeles, where his first recording session took place in 1951. He had a minor R&B hit for Bullet in 1952 with "Feelin' Sad," which was covered by Ray Charles. Charles also produced and played on Slim's later recordings.

Guitar Slim's mid-1950s Specialty recordings are generally considered his best work, although his biggest hit was 1945's "The Things That I Used to Do." Melding a swampy mood with churchy chords, this future blues standard spent weeks at No. 1 on the R&B charts, selling more than a million copies. On the strength of this song, he sold out an entire week of shows at Harlem's Apollo Theater, something even Sammy Davis Jr. wasn't able to do at the time.

Despite making high-quality records, he never charted again. Alcohol abuse and a string of bad life choices wore him down over the years and he died of pneumonia.

Slim's outrageous performance style influenced Jimi Hendrix. Frank Zappa and blues greats Albert Collins and Buddy Guy all cite Slim as a crucial influence.

TRIVIA: Slim claimed "The Things That I Used to Do" came to him in a dream.

GUITAR SLIM

SLIM HARPO

(JAMES MOORE)

MAIN INSTRUMENTS: Vocals, harmonica
BORN: Lobdell, Louisiana; January 11, 1924
DIED: Baton Rouge, Louisiana; January 31, 1970

RECOMMENDED TRACKS: "I'm a King Bee," "I Got Love If You Want It," "Rainin' in My Heart," "Baby Scratch My Back," "Shake Your Hips"

INTERESTING COVERS: "I'm a King Bee" (Rolling Stones), "I Got Love If You Want It" (Yardbirds, Kinks, High Numbers—a.k.a. the Who), "(Baby) Scratch My Back" (Fabulous Thunderbirds, Tony Joe White, Otis Redding, Yardbirds as "Rack My Mind" with new lyrics), "Shake Your Hips" (Rolling Stones), "Rainin' in My Heart" (Pretty Things)

The deaths of his parents left James Moore and his younger siblings orphans. He dropped out of school and worked as a longshoreman and in construction during the late 1930s and early '40s. At night he played every juke joint, fish fry, street corner, and party he could find, then picked up gigs in Baton Rouge bars under the name Harmonica Slim. James led the 1950s Louisiana swamp blues movement, pairing with brother-in-law Lightnin' Slim at gigs and in the studio before going completely solo in 1957.

He was named Slim Harpo by either his wife or producer Jay Miller. His solo debut, "I'm a King Bee"/"I Got Love If You Want It," was a double-sided R&B hit for Excello Records. Influenced by Jimmy Reed, he enjoyed a string of hit Excello R&B singles that combined a sensual, laid-back-in-the-extreme vocal with distinctive harmonica. Slim's R&B standard "Rainin' in My Heart" made the Billboard Top 40 pop charts in 1961.

Harpo enjoyed his biggest U.S. Top 20 pop hit (and No. 1 R&B hit) in 1966 with "Baby Scratch My Back."

Music was always a side job to Slim; he owned a trucking business during the 1960s. Suddenly, for the first time in his musical life, Harpo was in demand from coast to coast. At his peak, he reunited with Lightnin' Slim and toured to enthusiastic white rock audiences and was a popular figure in the late-1960s blues revival, with gigs that included the Electric Circus and the Fillmore East.

In early 1970 he had his first tour of Europe all ready to go, with a recording gig lined up after his London arrival. Harpo, who had been remarkably healthy his entire life, suddenly died from a heart attack.

SLIM HARPO

WYNONIE HARRIS

MAIN INSTRUMENTS: Vocals, drums
BORN: Omaha, Nebraska; August 24, 1915
DIED: Los Angeles, California; June 14, 1969

RECOMMENDED TRACKS: "Hurry Hurry," "Wynonie's Blues," "Playful Baby," "Young Man's Blues," "Around the Clock," "Good Rockin' Tonight"

INTERESTING COVERS: "Around the Clock" (Big Joe Turner, Jimmy Rushing, Chuck Berry as "Reelin' and Rockin'"), "Good Rockin' Tonight" (Elvis Presley)

As a teen, Wynonie Harris dropped out of school in Omaha and fathered two children with different women. At age twenty he wedded his sixteen-year-old girlfriend, then sang and took odd jobs for a living. By 1935 he was supporting himself as a dancer.

In 1940, Wynonie and his wife moved to Los Angeles, where he quickly found work singing and emceeing on the city's vibrant Central Avenue. He became known as "Mr. Blues."

The wartime shellac shortage (shellac was an ingredient crucial to the production of records) rendered most recording futile, so Wynonie devoted himself to nearly nonstop live performing. Spotted by Lucky Millinder at Chicago's Rhumboogie Café in 1943, he debuted with Lucky and his orchestra at Harlem's Apollo Theater and they recorded "Who Threw the Whiskey in the Well" for Decca. When it finally came out in 1945, it became their biggest hit, a Billboard R&B No. 1 that remained on the charts for nearly five months and was a rare crossover hit popular with both black and white record buyers. Harris's popularity grew as the orchestra toured, but Wynonie quit after he and Lucky had a financial falling out.

In 1945, Johnny Otis and his band backed Harris on his hit "Around the Clock." After he signed with King Records in 1947, his sales really took off. He originally turned down composer Roy Brown's offer to record "Good Rockin' Tonight," Harris covered it after Brown's version became a hit. Harris's 1948 version topped the charts and foreshadowed the rise of rock 'n' roll.

From 1946 to 1952 Wynonie couldn't miss, scoring fifteen Top 10 hits before his career crashed because of changing tastes. His record sales sank, the touring slowed, and he fell into debt. By 1963 he was scraping for low-paying gigs. A promising Chess session was never released. His last major gig was in 1967 at the Apollo. Cancer of the esophagus ended the life of this R&B pioneer.

TRIVIA: In 1946, Harris recorded a few songs with pianist Herman "Sonny" Blount, who later gained fame as the unusual jazz composer and bandleader Sun Ra.

WYNONIE HARRIS

SCREAMIN' JAY HAWKINS

(JALACY HAWKINS)

MAIN INSTRUMENTS: Vocals, piano
BORN: Cleveland, Ohio; July 18, 1929
DIED: Paris, France; February 12, 2000

RECOMMENDED TRACKS: "I Put a Spell on You," "Constipation Blues," "Feast of the Mau Mau," "Little Demon"

INTERESTING COVERS: "I Put a Spell on You" (Crazy World of Arthur Brown, Nina Simone, Manfred Mann, Alan Price, Them, Pete Townshend, Animals, Bryan Ferry, Creedence Clearwater Revival—the latter was Jay's favorite cover version)

Hawkins was taught classical piano as a child; he learned guitar in his early twenties. When he realized his dream of becoming a Paul Robeson–style opera singer was not an option, he reinvented himself as a blues singer and pianist.

Jay entertained the troops during his Pacific theater stint in the U.S. Army during WWII. According to Hawkins, he was captured and tortured as a POW. Jay's 1952 solo recording debut was "Why Did You Waste My Time," backed by Tiny Grimes and His Rockin' Highlanders (their stage wear included kilts and tams).

Hawkins hit big with his timeless "I Put a Spell on You" in 1956. His bigger-than-life stage character wore leopard-skin costumes and bizarre hats and used voodoo props like rubber snakes and a smoking skull-on-a-stick named Henry. He arose from a coffin onstage, a stunt that disc jockey Alan Freed first offered him $300 to do. Decreed "the black Vincent Price," Jay toured and recorded throughout the 1960s and '70s, being especially popular in Europe. He played himself in the 1978 film story on Alan Freed, *American Hot Wax*, and a hotel night clerk in Jim Jarmusch's 1989 cult favorite, *Mystery Train*.

Screamin' Jay Hawkins's over-the-top performances influenced rockers Arthur Brown, Alice Cooper, and Marilyn Manson. In the early 1990s, Jay toured with the Clash and Nick Cave. In addition to performing at blues festivals, he appeared at many film festivals. Jay died in Paris following surgery to treat an aneurysm.

TRIVIA: Jay left behind many children by many women—about fifty-seven offspring were known (or suspected) upon his death; as many as eighteen more were revealed after further inquiry. Jay also had an encyclopedic knowledge of and an eidetic memory for R&B musicians from the 1950s. He was the 1949 middleweight boxing champion of Alaska.

SCREAMIN' JAY HAWKINS

ROSA HENDERSON

(ROSA DESCHAMPS)

MAIN INSTRUMENT: Vocals
BORN: Henderson, Kentucky; November 24, 1896
DIED: Roosevelt Island, New York, New York; April 6, 1968

RECOMMENDED TRACKS: "Back Woods Blues," "Rough House Blues," "My Papa Doesn't Two-Time No Time," "Strut Yo' Puddy," "Nobody Knows the Way I Feel Dis Mornin'," "Chicago Policemen Blues," "Slow Up Papa"

At age seventeen, Rosa Deschamps began her show business career as one of her uncle's circus entertainers. She lived in Texas until 1918, when she married Douglas "Slim" Henderson, and then she continued touring. After moving to New York, she found work in the early 1920s in Broadway musical comedies and occasionally appeared in London. She recorded for just nine years, beginning in 1923. Henderson waxed eighty-eight songs from 1923 to 1927; then two apiece in 1928 and 1931 between performances. Her use of multiple pseudonyms—Rosa Green, Bessie Williams, Sally Ritz, Flora Dale, Sarah Johnson, Josephine Thomas, Gladys White, and Mamie Harris—contributed to her obscurity.

Rosa was backed by sidemen such as Coleman Hawkins and Fats Waller as well as by a variety of bands, including three led by Fletcher Henderson (no relation). It's likely her vocal on Henderson's 1924 Vocalion single "Do That Thing" is the first recording of a woman singing with a big band.

At the end of the 1920s Rosa began to drift out of the music scene, but she occasionally performed into the mid-1930s. She worked in a New York department store and in other nonmusic jobs, surfacing from time to time as a singer for charity benefits through the 1960s.

ROSA HENDERSON

BERTHA "CHIPPIE" HILL

MAIN INSTRUMENT: Vocals

BORN: Charleston, South Carolina; March 15, 1905
DIED: New York, New York; May 7, 1950

RECOMMENDED TRACKS: "Trouble in Mind," "Pratt City Blues," "Low Land Blues," "Weary Money Blues," "Christmas Man Blues," "Hard Times Blues"

INTERESTING COVERS: "Trouble in Mind" (Nina Simone, Dinah Washington, Jerry Lee Lewis, Muddy Waters, Janis Joplin, Mose Allison, Bob Wills and His Texas Playboys, Sam Cooke, Aretha Franklin, Les Paul, B.B. King, Big Joe Turner)

Bertha Hill was one of sixteen children. In 1915 her family moved to New York. The following year she began her career as a Harlem dancer, and by 1919 she was sharing the stage with Ethel Waters. Her youth got her the nickname of "Chippie." Hill toured with Ma Rainey before creating her own song-and-dance show. She worked the vaudeville and Theater Owners Booking Association circuit in the early 1920s, moving to Chicago in 1925 and singing with King Oliver's Jazz Band. Backed by Louis Armstrong and Richard M. Jones (she introduced his classic "Trouble in Mind"), her initial recordings were for OKeh in 1925. She also recorded with Scrapper Blackwell and the Two Roys (one of them being Leroy Carr), "Georgia Tom" Dorsey, Lovie Austin, and Montana Taylor and cut vocal duets with Lonnie Johnson and Tampa Red. Hill ultimately waxed twenty-three titles from 1925 through 1929.

After working steadily around Chicago, Chippie left the music business in 1930 to raise her seven children. For the next fifteen years she was mostly employed outside of music. In 1946, writer Rudi Blesh found her toiling in a bakery. After recording for Blesh's Circle label, she appeared on his *This Is Jazz* radio series, which resulted in her return to the music world with Lovie Austin's Blues Serenaders. Hill became one of the rare singers of her generation to make a full comeback in the 1940s, performing in 1948 at both Carnegie Hall with Kid Ory and the Paris Jazz Festival.

Chippie remained at the top of her game until she was hit by a car and killed.

BERTHA "CHIPPIE" HILL

BILLIE HOLIDAY

(ELEANORA HARRIS)

MAIN INSTRUMENT: Vocals
BORN: Baltimore, Maryland; April 7, 1915
DIED: New York, New York; July 17, 1959

RECOMMENDED TRACKS: "Long Gone Blues," "'Tain't Nobody's Business If I Do,"
"God Bless the Child," "Lady Sings the Blues," "Billie's Blues," "Strange Fruit"

INTERESTING COVERS: "Strange Fruit" (Nina Simone), "God Bless the Child" (Steve
Miller; Blood, Sweat, and Tears)

Teen guitarist Clarence Halliday (Holiday) abandoned Billie as a baby. She was raped by a neighbor at age ten. She and her mom moved to New York in 1928, where Billie sang in Harlem clubs for tips, did domestic work, and moonlighted as a prostitute. After imprisonment for solicitation she returned to club work. Her stage name came from actress Billie Dove. Columbia's John Hammond reviewed her for *Melody Maker* in 1933 and brought Benny Goodman to see her. She recorded with Benny and established herself as a major vocalist. In 1937, she recorded and toured with members of the Count Basie Orchestra. As Artie Shaw's vocalist, Billie was one of the first black women to work with a white orchestra. Sponsors and promoters of Shaw's gigs, however, objected to Holiday's singing style and her race. Shaw stuck up for her, but racist indignities perpetrated against Billie grew until she quit after being asked to use the service elevator instead of the passenger elevator. Hammond refused to record the racially charged "Strange Fruit" for Columbia but allowed its Commodore release. Banned from the radio, the song became a jukebox hit. Billie married drug smuggler Jimmie Monroe in 1941. That same year, Holiday's popular self-penned song "God Bless the Child" earned her access to better material.

In 1947 Billie divorced Monroe and married trumpeter Joe Guy, who supplied her with heroin. She split with Guy that same year. Most of her money went to feed her drug habit. A drug bust sentenced her to prison for a year and got her banned from New York clubs for the rest of her life. A 1948 Carnegie Hall comeback concert resulted in a record 2,700-ticket sellout. In 1957 she married Mafia enforcer Louis McKay, who tried to clean her up. She collapsed from heart and liver disease in 1959. Still using heroin while on her hospital deathbed, Billie was arrested and remained under police guard until she died from cirrhosis.

TRIVIA: Billie died with just seventy cents in the bank.

BILLIE HOLIDAY

EARL HOOKER

MAIN INSTRUMENTS: Guitar, vocals, drums, piano, banjo, mandolin
BORN: Clarksdale, Mississippi; January 15, 1929
DIED: Chicago, Illinois; April 21, 1970

RECOMMENDED TRACKS: "Drivin' Wheel," "Catfish Blues," "Crosscut Saw," "Sweet Home Chicago," "You Don't Want Me," "Sweet Black Angel," "Blue Guitar"

INTERESTING COVERS: "You Shook Me" (Jeff Beck Group, Led Zeppelin), "Sweet Black Angel" (Jeff Beck Group as "Sweet Little Angel"), "Drivin' Wheel" (Paul Butterfield Blues Band)

The family of John Lee Hooker's cousin Earl Zebedee Hooker moved to Chicago when he was one. He taught himself guitar at age ten, then formally studied the drums, piano, banjo, and mandolin at music school. Earl ran away from home at age thirteen, returning briefly to Mississippi. Back in Chicago, the teen played street corners with his childhood pal Bo Diddley. Earl's interest in slide guitar developed from his performing friendship with Robert Nighthawk, who taught Earl various tunings and techniques. In 1949, Hooker moved to Memphis, joined Ike Turner's band, and toured the South. Earl performed with Sonny Boy Williamson II (Rice Miller) and joined him on his *King Biscuit Time* radio program between Nighthawk gigs. In the mid-1950s, Earl Hooker led his own Chicago-based band. Hooker's first recordings were in 1952; a year later he recorded with Pinetop Perkins at Sun. Earl backed Junior Wells and many others throughout his career. His solo recordings were mostly instrumentals. Hooker's "Blue Guitar" became the backing track for Muddy Waters's 1962 classic "You Shook Me." Earl recorded for the small Cuca label from 1964 to 1968. His 1965 European tour included a spot on England's pop music TV show *Ready, Steady, Go!*

Hooker spent the end of the 1960s playing Chicago clubs with his band and Junior Wells. He popularized oddities like the double-neck guitar and the wah-wah pedal as featured on—what else?—"Wah Wah Blues." Earl's 1969 LP *Hooker 'n' Steve*, recorded with organist Steve "Mr. Blues" Miller (not the famed guitarist) for Arhoolie, as well as his subsequent records, helped spread his fame beyond his Chicago audiences. His last LP, 1969's *Sweet Black Angel,* was coproduced by Ike Turner. Hooker died from tuberculosis soon after its recording, exhilarated yet dramatically weakened by touring Europe with the American Folk Blues Festival.

TRIVIA: Jimi Hendrix proclaimed Earl Hooker the "master of the wah-wah."

EARL HOOKER

JOHN LEE HOOKER

(A.K.A. HOOK)

MAIN INSTRUMENTS: Guitar, vocals
BORN: Coahoma County (near Clarksdale), Mississippi; August 22, 1917
DIED: Los Altos, California; June 21, 2001

RECOMMENDED TRACKS: "Boom Boom," "Crawling King Snake," "Maudie," "I'm in the Mood," "Dimples"

INTERESTING COVERS: "Boom Boom" (Animals), "Crawling King Snake" (Eric Burdon), "Maudie" (Animals), "Dimples" (Spencer Davis Group)

John Lee Hooker, Earl's cousin, was the youngest of eleven musical kids who were homeschooled by their sharecropping Baptist preacher father and allowed to listen to only religious songs. After his parents separated in 1921, John's mother married blues singer William Moore, who taught Hooker a one-chord blues drone guitar style different from that period's Delta blues. John transformed this style into his own unique blues genre called "the boogie." His highly personal playing changed tempo and added bars to fit his whims, which made backing him difficult.

In Memphis during the 1930s, he worked Beale Street and played house parties. He landed a Ford job in 1948. Good guitarists were scarce in Detroit, and John's popularity quickly grew. When the high noise level in clubs necessitated a louder instrument, T-Bone Walker came to the rescue, giving John Lee his first electric guitar.

Hook's prolific recording career kicked off in 1948 with "Boogie Chillen'," the first of many hits; he ultimately made more than one hundred LPs. To get around exclusivity clauses, he recorded for various labels as Texas Slim, Delta John, John Lee Booker, Birmingham Sam, Little Pork Chops, Johnny Williams, Boogie Man, and Johnny Lee before he finally settled in at Vee-Jay in 1955 under his own name.

British bands loved him. The Animals' 1964 "Boom Boom" cover outsold his original. Hooker toured Europe in 1962 with the first American Folk Blues Festival. Teaming with Canned Heat for their 1970 hit LP, *Hooker 'n' Heat*, greatly expanded his popularity. John Lee's guest-star-packed album *The Healer* won a 1989 Best Traditional Blues Grammy. He spent his final years in Long Beach, California. He fell ill just before a 2001 European tour and died soon after of natural causes.

TRIVIA: John Lee Hooker sang in the 1980 movie *The Blues Brothers*. In 1989, Pete Townshend cast him as the title character in *The Iron Man: A Musical*.

JOHN LEE HOOKER

LIGHTNIN' HOPKINS

(SAM HOPKINS)

MAIN INSTRUMENTS: Guitar, vocals
BORN: Centerville, Texas; March 15, 1912
DIED: Houston, Texas; January 30, 1982

RECOMMENDED TRACKS: "Katie May," "Shotgun Blues," "Mojo Hand," "T-Model Blues," "Tim Moore's Farm," "Give Me Central 209," "Coffee Blues"

Sam Hopkins's love for the blues struck him at age eight, when he met Blind Lemon Jefferson at a Buffalo, Texas, church picnic. He became Lemon's guide and began to learn from him and support him on guitar at church events. Sam's cousins, blues singers "Texas" Alexander and Frankie Lee Sims, also tutored Hopkins. In the mid-1930s Hopkins landed at the Houston County Prison Farm (offense unknown) and then moved to Houston and reconnected with Alexander. Unable to make it musically, in the early 1940s he labored as a Centerville farmhand and played with Alexander on weekends.

In 1946 an Aladdin talent scout saw promise in Hopkins's rustic blues. She teamed him with pianist Wilson "Thunder" Smith and renamed Sam "Lightnin'." His first regional seller was 1946's "Katie May." He recorded at nearly every opportunity through 1948, hitting big on the R&B charts with "Shotgun Blues." From the late 1940s to the '50s, Hopkins performed on rare occasions in the Midwest and East, but mostly limited himself to Houston-area clubs. He recorded a staggering number of songs (eight hundred to a thousand!) during his career, however. By the late 1950s, his enormous output of high-quality material had achieved him a strong national following.

In 1959 Hopkins played to integrated audiences as a folk-blues artist in Houston and California. The following year, he debuted at Carnegie Hall, performing with Joan Baez and Pete Seeger, and recorded his masterpiece, "Mojo Hand." He continued to build renown as a compelling blues performer throughout the 1960s.

He recorded the 1968 LP *Free Form Patterns* with the rhythm section of the infamously psychedelic Thirteenth Floor Elevators. Throughout the 1960s and '70s, Lightnin' released one or more albums a year while touring major folk festivals and clubs and campuses all over the world. One of the few remaining country blues giants, Lightnin' Hopkins successfully united rural and urban styles.

TRIVIA: Lightnin' Hopkins recorded more albums than any other bluesman. Filmmaker Les Blank skillfully presented his life in his lauded 1967 documentary *The Blues Accordin' to Lightnin' Hopkins*.

LIGHTNIN' HOPKINS

WALTER "SHAKEY" HORTON

(A.K.A. BIG WALTER HORTON, SHAKEY WALTER, MUMBLES)

MAIN INSTRUMENT: Harmonica
BORN: Horn Lake, Mississippi; April 6, 1917
DIED: Chicago, Illinois; December 8, 1981

RECOMMENDED TRACKS: "Walking by Myself" (backing Jimmy Rogers), "Easy" (with Jimmy DeBerry), "I Can't Quit You Baby" (backing Otis Rush)

INTERESTING COVER: "I Can't Quit You Baby" (Led Zeppelin)

Walter Horton began playing harmonica at age five and spent his early teens in Memphis, Tennessee, playing for tips. He claimed that he first recorded in the 1920s with the Memphis Jug Band (maybe) and that he trained Little Walter and Sonny Boy Williamson (doubtful). He learned licks from the Jug Band's Will Shade. Horton—known as "Shakey" because of the way he moved his head while he played—performed at dances, parties, juke joints, and on the streets during the Depression. He paired with Robert Johnson, Homesick James, and David "Honeyboy" Edwards; toured with the Ma Rainey and Big Joe Williams bands; and briefly played Chicago. His first records were likely made in Memphis in 1939. Horton claimed he experimented with harp amplification at that time. If true, he may have been the first. Poor health curtailed his playing during most of the 1940s. By the 1950s, he was back in Chicago.

Horton replaced Junior Wells (who had been drafted) on a 1952 Muddy Waters session. A Chess session man, he also cut his own singles for various labels. His solo on Jimmy Rogers's "Walking by Myself" is a Chicago blues treasure.

From the early 1960s on, Walter backed many blues stars. His own LPs didn't capture his talents. However, Vanguard's 1967 LP, *Chicago/The Blues/Today! Volume 3*, plugged him in to the folk-blues revival circuit. Shakey joined Willie Dixon's Blues All Stars for American and European tours in the 1960s and '70s. He recorded with Fleetwood Mac in 1968. Horton tutored Charlie Musselwhite and Carey Bell, and recorded *Big Walter Horton with Carey Bell* in 1972. In 1977 he was tapped by Johnny Winter for Muddy Waters's *I'm Ready* LP. Heavy drinking and painful shyness (he preferred sideman work) kept Horton from becoming a big star on his own. Walter died of heart failure.

TRIVIA: Willie Dixon called Horton "the best harmonica player I ever heard." Walter accompanied John Lee Hooker in *The Blues Brothers*. His classic "Easy" was based on Ivory Joe Hunter's "I Almost Lost My Mind."

WALTER "SHAKEY" HORTON

HOWLIN' WOLF

(CHESTER ARTHUR BURNETT)

MAIN INSTRUMENTS: Vocals, harmonica, guitar
BORN: White Station, Mississippi; June 10, 1910
DIED: Hines, Illinois; January 10, 1976

RECOMMENDED TRACKS: "Evil," "Smokestack Lightnin'," "Sitting on Top of the World," "Wang Dang Doodle," "Back Door Man," "Killing Floor," "Spoonful," "I Ain't Superstitious," "No Place to Go," "Little Red Rooster"

INTERESTING COVERS: "Sitting on Top of the World" (Cream), "Smokestack Lightnin'" (Manfred Mann, Animals, Yardbirds), "Wang Dang Doodle" (Love Sculpture), "Spoonful" (Cream, Paul Butterfield Blues Band), "Back Door Man" (Doors), "I Ain't Superstitious" (Jeff Beck Group), "Killing Floor" (Electric Flag, Led Zeppelin as "The Lemon Song"), "No Place to Go" (Led Zeppelin as "How Many More Times"), "Little Red Rooster" (Sam Cooke)

At six foot six and about three hundred pounds, Howlin' Wolf had presence. His stage name came from his grandfather, who warned that if Chester was bad, the howlin' wolves would "get him." Chester learned guitar from Charley Patton and harp from Sonny Boy Williamson II, who married Wolf's half-sister. By 1948 he had a radio show and his own band, in which Willie Johnson's aggressive guitar intensified Wolf's violent, nasty sound.

Wolf auditioned in 1951 for Sam Phillips, who leased Wolf's first efforts to Modern and Chess Records—both at the same time. They scored hits before Wolf ever set foot in Chicago. Chess ultimately won out. Wolf arrived in Chicago with $3,900 cash and a new car due to his Memphis recording and performing success and his ability to resist the typical temptations of the blues life. This put him in an excellent negotiating position with Chess. He was illiterate until he was in his forties, when he returned to school, earned a GED, and took business and accounting courses. Wolf's ability to offer his band good pay and health insurance enabled him to hire the best players.

The Rolling Stones covered his "Little Red Rooster," which hit No. 1 in England. In 1965 the Stones agreed to be on the ABC pop music show *Shindig*, but only if Howlin' Wolf appeared as their guest. Thanks to the Stones, Wolf's TV debut had millions of viewers.

Howlin' Wolf survived heart attacks, but suffered kidney damage in a car accident. He entered a V.A. hospital for a kidney operation, but didn't survive.

TRIVIA: Howlin' Wolf's given name, Chester Arthur, honored the twenty-first president of the United States. Wolf was honored with a U.S. postage stamp in 1994.

HOWLIN' WOLF

HELEN HUMES

MAIN INSTRUMENT: Vocals
BORN: Louisville, Kentucky; June 23, 1913
DIED: Santa Monica, California; September 9, 1981

RECOMMENDED TRACKS: "Airplane Blues," "Fortune Tellin' Man," "He May Be Your Man," "Be-Baba-Leba," "Do What You Did Last Night," "Million Dollar Secret," "Today I Sing the Blues," "'Tain't Nobody's Biz-ness If I Do"

Helen Humes was spotted playing church keyboards by local guitarist Sylvester Weaver. She recorded ten blues songs when she was only thirteen, her young voice taking on mature material like "Garlic Blues." Humes evolved into a sassy R&B diva and a seasoned interpreter of the finest popular songs and swing standards. She moved to New York in 1937 and recorded with Harry James.

The following year, Humes became a vocalist with Count Basie, replacing Billie Holiday as his lead female singer. Since Basie singer Jimmy Rushing specialized in blues, Helen was relegated to singing pop ballads, which she did with taste and passion. After playing a variety of gigs in New York and touring from the early to mid-1940s, Humes settled in Los Angeles. She had a solo hit with 1945's "Be-Baba-Leba," and "Million Dollar Secret" from 1950 is considered a classic. Humes occasionally participated in Jazz at the Philharmonic and worked solo as well as with many bands and singers, including Nat King Cole.

She toured and recorded three great LPs from 1959 to 1961 and appeared at the 1960 Monterey Jazz Festival. Helen moved to Hawaii and then Australia in the mid-1960s, returning to the U.S. mainland in 1967 to take care of her mother. She left showbiz for several years and then made a dramatic comeback at the Newport Jazz Festival in 1973. She sang all over Europe, working right up until her death from cancer.

Humes started her career as a salty blues artist, but eventually bridged the gap between big-band jazz swing and R&B. Her public never lost its passion for her blues vocals, but perhaps her greatest strength was as a balladeer.

HELEN HUMES

ALBERTA HUNTER

MAIN INSTRUMENT: Vocals
BORN: Memphis, Tennessee; April 1, 1895
DIED: New York, New York; October 17, 1984

RECOMMENDED TRACK: "Downhearted Blues"

INTERESTING COVERS: "Downhearted Blues" (Bessie Smith, Janis Joplin)

Born to a servant in a Memphis whorehouse, Alberta Hunter left for Chicago circa 1911 after hearing that singers there earned ten bucks a week. Instead, she landed a job at a boardinghouse for six bucks a week plus room and food. Skinning potatoes by day and pestering club owners by night, her perseverance lifted her from bawdy houses to a five-year headlining gig at Chicago's most prestigious black venue. Her salary rose to thirty-five dollars a week. She married twice, despite her preference for women.

After a stray bullet killed her piano man, Alberta moved to New York City, where she recorded Black Swan Records' first blues vocal. Black Swan was acquired by Paramount, for which Hunter wrote "Downhearted Blues." Secretly selling Columbia the rights (while keeping most of the royalties), producer Ink Williams gave Alberta just $368 for the song, which was the first to be recorded by Bessie Smith and became a huge hit. Hunter dropped Williams and Paramount and recorded more than eighty songs before 1930, often under pseudonyms like Josephine Beatty, Alberta Prime, Anna Jones, and May Alix. She also starred as Queenie opposite Paul Robeson in the premier London production of *Show Boat* in 1928.

Hunter first toured Europe in 1917, and she stayed there during the Depression. Back home, her meager results in the 1940s for records with sketchy indie labels were in direct contrast to her success on the USO circuit during and after WWII.

After her mother's death in 1954, Alberta lied about her age, faked a high school diploma, entered nursing school, and began a new career as a New York hospital nurse. She reentered showbiz in 1961 with *Songs We Taught Your Mother* but later resumed nursing until the hospital, believing she was sixty-five, retired her in 1977, when she was eighty-one! Bored, Hunter returned to singing in 1978. Her two weeks at the Cookery in Greenwich Village were so popular that it became an open-ended run. Alberta continued to perform until her death.

TRIVIA: Invited to sing at the White House, Alberta turned the gig down because "they wanted me there on my day off." The White House rearranged its schedule.

ALBERTA HUNTER

ELMORE JAMES

(ELMORE BROOKS)

MAIN INSTRUMENTS: Guitar, vocals
BORN: Richland, Mississippi; January 27, 1918
DIED: Chicago, Illinois; May 24, 1963

RECOMMENDED TRACKS: "Dust My Broom," "The Sky Is Crying," "Stranger Blues," "Look on Yonder Wall," "Done Somebody Wrong," "Shake Your Moneymaker"

INTERESTING COVERS: "Dust My Broom" (Fleetwood Mac), "The Sky Is Crying" (Etta James, Stevie Ray Vaughan), "Shake Your Moneymaker" (Fleetwood Mac), "Done Somebody Wrong" (Allman Brothers Band), "One Way Out" (Allman Brothers Band)

INTERESTING TRIBUTE: "No More Elmore" (Eric Burdon)

Elmore James, "King of the Slide Guitar," was the son of a fifteen-year-old unmarried field hand. He began making music on a homemade one-string "diddley bow," or "jitterbug," when he was twelve. At fourteen he performed at dances as "Joe Willie James" and "Cleanhead." He worked with touring players like Robert Johnson, Sonny Boy Williamson II, and Howlin' Wolf, touring the South with Sonny Boy until WWII. After the war, Elmore worked in a Canton, Mississippi, radio repair shop. He used shop parts to alter his guitar and gear to emit original, biting, distorted sounds, predating rock amplification effects.

James moved to Memphis, where he worked with his cousin Homesick James and with Eddie Taylor. Elmore was a regular guest on Sonny Boy's *King Biscuit Time* radio show and other programs. James's career was a lifelong series of stops and starts due to a fragile heart condition and his fondness for moonshine whiskey. He was unsure of his own recording abilities, so Trumpet Records secretly taped his "Dust My Broom" at the end of a Sonny Boy session. The unexpected 1951 Top 10 R&B hit made James a star. Several of James's blues classics charted in the 1950s. In 1959 he began recording many of what would become his most famous songs with a series of singles for Fire Records. He returned to Mississippi, then traveled to New York and New Orleans. Back in Chicago, he resumed his on-again, off-again music career, and he died from his third heart attack.

Elmore James's work influenced nearly every postwar slide guitar player. Fleetwood Mac's Jeremy Spencer used to begin most of his live songs with Elmore's signature opening lick to "Dust My Broom."

TRIVIA: Jimi Hendrix originally named himself "Maurice James" and "Jimmy James" in tribute to Elmore. During his slide solo in "For You Blue," Beatle George Harrison boasts, "Elmore James got nothin' on this, baby."

ELMORE JAMES

SKIP JAMES

(NEHEMIAH CURTIS JAMES)

MAIN INSTRUMENTS: Vocals, guitar, piano
BORN: Near Bentonia, Mississippi; June 21, 1902
DIED: Philadelphia, Pennsylvania; October 3, 1969

RECOMMENDED TRACKS: "I'm So Glad," "Hard Time Killing Floor Blues," "Cherry Ball Blues," "Devil Got My Woman," "Jesus Is a Mighty Good Leader"

INTERESTING COVERS: "I'm So Glad" (Cream, Deep Purple), "Jesus Is a Mighty Good Leader" (Beck as "He's a Mighty Good Leader"), "Hard Time Killing Floor Blues" (Chris Thomas King)

S kip James learned to play the organ in his teens. In the 1920s, he worked on Mississippi construction crews, sharecropped, and bootlegged whiskey. Little Brother Montgomery inspired his guitar and piano playing. In 1931, on the strength of a Jackson, Mississippi, audition, James recorded for Paramount in Wisconsin, often combining musical genres and sources. "I'm So Glad" came from the 1927 Art Sizemore and George A. Little song "So Tired," recorded in 1928 by Lonnie Johnson as "I'm So Tired of Livin' All Alone." James changed the lyrics and transformed the song with his elegant guitar technique and vocals. Of the twenty-six recordings Skip made for Paramount, only eighteen survive.

During the Great Depression, James's records sold poorly. He became the choir director at his father's church and was ordained as both a Baptist and a Methodist minister. He stopped recording for more than thirty years, becoming virtually unknown. In 1964, blues fans found him in a Mississippi hospital. According to James's biographer, Stephen Calt, the simultaneous resurfacing of Skip James and Son House ignited the 1960s American blues revival. James performed a revelatory set at the Newport Folk Festival in 1964.

Skip rarely socialized and held the 1960s folkie scene in contempt. He thought highly of his own work but was not enthusiastic to share what he knew with others. He embodied the contradictory psyche common to many bluesmen who lived tough, incautious existences while still espousing strict religious dogma.

The royalties from Cream's versions of "I'm So Glad" (which Skip considered a children's song) provided James with the only good fortune of his career. The money extended James's life, paying for some sorely needed medical care.

TRIVIA: "Devil Got My Woman" was featured in the plot of Terry Zwigoff's 2001 *Ghost World*. Singer Dion DiMucci's 2007 album was entitled *Son of Skip James*. James's "22-20 Blues" became more famous as "32-20 Blues" by Robert Johnson.

SKIP JAMES

FRANKIE "HALF PINT" JAXON

MAIN INSTRUMENT: Vocals
BORN: Montgomery, Alabama; February 3, 1895 (or 1897)
DIED: Los Angeles, California (?); 1944 or 1970

RECOMMENDED TRACKS: "Willie the Weeper," "Fan It," "How Long How Long Blues," "It's Tight Like That"

INTERESTING COVERS: "Willie the Weeper" (Cab Calloway as "Minnie the Moocher"), "Fan It" (Woody Herman, Red Nichols)

Frankie "Half Pint" (he was five feet two) Jaxon grew up as an orphan in Kansas City, Missouri. By fifteen, he was performing in clubs and variety shows. He toured with medicine shows and a theatrical troupe in Texas and Oklahoma and from 1912 to 1924 he led a successful vaudeville song-and-dance team.

In 1917 Jaxon began working summers at Atlantic City's Paradise Café and winters at Chicago's Sunset Café. His sweet, high voice and flamboyant stage presence, with him often in drag, made him very popular. Well studied in theatrical presentation, Half Pint helped Bessie Smith, Ethel Waters, and others stage and design their productions. At the end of the 1920s he sang with King Oliver and other important jazz bands when their tours took them through Chicago. He played with Cow Cow Davenport, Tampa Red, and "Georgia Tom" Dorsey, recording with the latter two as the Black Hillbillies.

Working as a saxophonist and singing pianist—and a female impersonator—Jaxon performed and recorded in Chicago from 1927 to 1941. In 1930 he put together the Quarts of Joy, and Jaxon often found himself appearing on the radio during the 1930s. Half Pint put out recordings as a bandleader from 1926 to 1940, on which sidemen like Georgia Tom, the Harlem Hamfats, and Lil Armstrong played. His composition "Fan It" was his signature tune. While still quite popular, Jaxon suddenly and mysteriously dropped out of music to work at the Pentagon in Washington, D.C., in 1941. He was transferred to Los Angeles in 1944 and disappeared. Most accounts state that he died in the veterans' hospital; other reports indicate he lived in Los Angeles until 1970.

Most of his recordings exhibit the ribald comedy and double entendres of hokum. His sensual parodies of "How Long How Long Blues" and "It's Tight Like That" are hilarious.

TRIVIA: Jaxon starred with Duke Ellington in the short "soundie" film *Black and Tan Fantasy* (1929). Cab Calloway's "Minnie the Moocher" (1931) is based both musically and lyrically on Jaxon's "Willie the Weeper" (1927).

FRANKIE HALF PINT JAXON

LONNIE JOHNSON

(ALONZO JOHNSON)

MAIN INSTRUMENTS: Guitar, vocals
BORN: New Orleans, Louisiana; February 8, 1899
DIED: Toronto, Ontario; June 16, 1970

RECOMMENDED TRACKS: "Tomorrow Night," "He's a Jelly Roll Baker," "In Love Again," "Pleasing You (As Long as I Live)," "Confused," "So Tired"

INTERESTING COVERS: "Tomorrow Night" (Elvis Presley, Jerry Lee Lewis)

Johnson studied violin, piano, and guitar and played in his father's family band. Lonnie toured England with a musical revue in 1917. Upon returning home two years later, he found that, except for his brother James, his entire family had perished from the Spanish flu. He and James moved to St. Louis and worked as a duo while Lonnie also played the riverboats. In 1925 he won an OKeh recording contract in a theater blues contest. He made about 130 recordings between 1925 and 1932, but the versatile guitarist found it difficult to transcend the limits of being labeled a blues artist.

Johnson recorded in Chicago with Louis Armstrong and His Hot Five in 1927 and with Duke Ellington in 1928. He played one of the first recorded guitar solos on "6/88 Glide" (1927), and his early twelve-string solos influenced jazz guitarists Charlie Christian and Django Reinhardt. With Eddie Lang disguised as Blind Willie Dunn, they made some of the first biracial recordings in 1928 and 1929. In New York, Lonnie recorded with Victoria Spivey and Texas Alexander, then toured with Bessie Smith.

During the Depression Lonnie worked in a Peoria steel mill. Using an electric guitar for the first time, he recorded thirty-four tracks for Bluebird from 1939 to 1944, including one of the biggest hits of his unusually long career, "Tomorrow Night." It topped the 1948 R&B charts for seven weeks. More hits followed.

Lonnie dropped out of music again in the 1950s and worked as a hotel janitor in Philadelphia. A disc jockey found him and produced the huge 1959 comeback LP *Blues by Lonnie Johnson*. In 1961, Johnson reunited with Duke Ellington, and then Spivey, and cut a series of LPs. He toured Europe with the American Folk Blues Festival and recorded a Danish LP with Otis Spann. In 1966, he opened his Home of the Blues club in Toronto and continued to record and tour. Lonnie was hit by a car in 1969. He never fully recovered from the accident and died a year later.

TRIVIA: In 1952, Johnson toured England. Tony Donegan, a British musician on the same bill, paid tribute to Johnson by changing his name to Lonnie Donegan.

LONNIE JOHNSON

PETE JOHNSON

MAIN INSTRUMENT: Piano
BORN: Kansas City, Missouri; March 25, 1904
DIED: Buffalo, New York; March 23, 1967

RECOMMENDED TRACKS: "Roll 'Em Pete," "Rocket 88 Boogie"

INTERESTING COVERS: "Roll 'Em Pete" (Jimmy Witherspoon, Jimmy Reed, Long John Baldry, Blasters, Lou Rawls, Bill Wyman's Rhythm Kings)

After beginning his musical career in Kansas City, Johnson switched from drums to piano in 1922. From 1926 to 1938, he often supported Big Joe Turner. Producer John Hammond discovered Pete in 1936 and got him important New York gigs. After appearing with Turner at Hammond's 1938 *From Spirituals to Swing* Carnegie Hall concert, Johnson recorded regularly, performing with Albert Ammons and Meade Lux Lewis as the Boogie Woogie Trio. They popularized boogie and were featured in the 1941 short *Boogie-Woogie Dream.*

Johnson recorded throughout the 1940s, living in Los Angeles throughout most of 1947 to 1949. "Roll 'Em Pete," featuring Big Joe Turner on vocals, was a pioneering rock 'n' roll record. Pete may have lifted the tune from Jelly Roll Morton, who often forgot to officially register his works. In 1949, Pete wrote and recorded "Rocket 88 Boogie," a forerunner to the 1951 Ike Turner hit "Rocket 88."

In the late 1940s, Johnson recorded the concept LP *House Rent Party*, which begins with Pete playing alone, but then he is gradually joined by other Kansas City musicians, each of whom performs a solo backed by Johnson before the entire group jams together.

In 1950 Johnson moved to Buffalo, New York. Despite health issues, including losing part of a finger while freeing his car from a snowbank, Pete toured and recorded with Big Joe and made the 1958 Jazz at the Philharmonic European tour. A post-tour stroke partially paralyzed him. Ill and broke, Johnson's last appearance was just two months prior to his death at a 1967 revival of John Hammond's *From Spirituals to Swing* concert idea, where he played the right-hand part of "Roll 'Em Pete."

TRIVIA: Each night at a Niagara Falls nightclub gig, Johnson had to climb a long ladder to get to the piano above the bar.

PETE JOHNSON

ROBERT JOHNSON

(ROBERT LEROY DODDS)

MAIN INSTRUMENTS: Guitar, vocals
BORN: Hazlehurst, Mississippi; May 8, 1911
DIED: Greenwood, Mississippi; August 16, 1938

RECOMMENDED TRACKS: "Crossroads Blues," "Love in Vain," "Have You Ever Been Lonely," "Hellhound on My Trail," "Stop Breakin' Down Blues," "From Four Until Late," "Traveling Riverside Blues," "Come On in My Kitchen"

INTERESTING COVERS: "Crossroads" (Cream), "Love in Vain" (Rolling Stones), "Hellhound on My Trail" (Fleetwood Mac), "Stop Breakin' Down Blues" (Rolling Stones), "From Four Until Late" (Cream), "Traveling Riverside Blues" (Led Zeppelin), "Come On in My Kitchen" (Delaney & Bonnie and Friends).

INTERESTING TRIBUTES: Eric Clapton and the Peter Green Splinter Group recorded two CDs each that cover all of Johnson's songs (of the two by Clapton, *Sessions for Robert J* is vastly superior and includes an interesting DVD). John Hammond and Todd Rundgren have also recorded Johnson tribute CDs.

Robert Leroy Johnson was born to Julia Dodds and Noah Johnson. A white lynch mob forced Julia's husband, Charles Dodds, to leave town over a dispute. Julia left home with Robert, but two years later shipped him off to live with Dodds (a.k.a. Charles Spencer) in Memphis. In 1919, Robert reunited with his mother and met her new husband, Dusty Willis, in Mississippi. As a skilled harmonica and jaw harp player, he became "Little Robert Dusty." After leaving school, Robert took his natural father's surname.

According to legend, young Robert held a burning desire to be a great blues musician. He was told to take his guitar to a local crossroads at midnight. He was met by a large, black man, the Devil, who tuned Johnson's guitar and handed it back to him in exchange for his soul. From that moment on, Robert could play, sing, and create the greatest blues ever heard.

When Johnson hit a new town, he'd play for tips on the street, adapting to his audience, performing jazz, country, and blues. Robert played sixteen selections at a three-day San Antonio recording session in 1936, returning home with more cash than he'd ever had at one time. In 1937, Johnson laid down thirteen more songs in a makeshift studio in Dallas. These twenty-nine landmark songs have profoundly influenced successive generations of musicians.

In the last year of his life, Robert Johnson is believed to have performed in St. Louis, Memphis, and throughout the Mississippi Delta. At age twenty-seven, he was poisoned by a jealous husband at a country dance.

ROBERT JOHNSON

BLIND WILLIE JOHNSON

(ALONZO JOHNSON)

MAIN INSTRUMENTS: Slide guitar, vocals
BORN: Near Brenham, Texas; January 22, 1897 (or 1902)
DIED: Beaumont, Texas; September 18, 1945

RECOMMENDED TRACKS: "Dark Was the Night—Cold Was the Ground," "Soul of a Man," "Nobody's Fault but Mine," "Jesus Make Up My Dying Bed"

INTERESTING COVERS: "Nobody's Fault but Mine" (Led Zeppelin, Nina Simone), "Dark Was the Night—Cold Was the Ground" (Ry Cooder), "Soul of a Man" (Eric Burdon), "John the Revelator" (White Stripes), "Jesus Make Up My Dying Bed" (Led Zeppelin as "In My Time of Dying")

When he was five, Willie Johnson informed his father of his desire to be a preacher, then fashioned a guitar out of a cigar box for himself.

Johnson was not born blind. Legend has it that when Willie was seven, as his father beat his cheating stepmother, she tossed a handful of lye that hit young Willie's eyes. Willie began earning money as a street busker, one of the few forms of employment open to a blind man. Despite his extraordinary slide guitar work, and his outstanding grasp of the blues, he had no desire to be considered a bluesman. A fervent Christian, he sang gospel, rearranged classic Negro spirituals, and eventually became a Baptist street preacher. While playing in Dallas, he met his second wife-to-be, Angeline, who added nineteenth-century hymns to his repertoire.

Willie became one of Columbia's bestselling black artists. Even though he made only thirty studio recordings during his five 1927 to 1930 Columbia sessions, many of them are gospel-blues classics. His first wife, Willie B. Harris, backs him vocally on fourteen of the tracks. Despite his robust sales, he mysteriously never heard from Columbia again. Johnson returned to playing the streets of Beaumont, Texas. In 1947, the Johnsons' home perished in a fire. With nowhere else to go, Willie took shelter in the ruins, sleeping on a wet bed. Weakened by syphilis, he contracted malarial fever and, just a few weeks after the fire, he died.

TRIVIA: Ry Cooder, who based his bleak *Paris, Texas* soundtrack on "Dark Was the Night—Cold Was the Ground," described that song, featuring Johnson's wordless hums and moans about the crucifixion of Jesus, as "the most soulful, transcendent piece in all American music." It was included on the Voyager Golden Record, which was sent into space with Voyagers 1 and 2 in 1977. Johnson's music left our solar system on December 15, 2004, and again on September 5, 2007.

BLIND WILLIE **JOHNSON**

LOUIS JORDAN

MAIN INSTRUMENTS: Vocals, saxophone, piano, clarinet
BORN: Brinkley, Arkansas; July 8, 1908
DIED: Los Angeles, California; February 4, 1975

RECOMMENDED TRACKS: "I'm Gonna Move to the Outskirts of Town," "Ration Blues," "Don't Let the Sun Catch You Crying," "Early in the Morning," "Keep A-Knockin'," "Let the Good Times Roll," "Choo Choo Ch'Boogie," "Caldonia"

INTERESTING COVERS: "Early in the Morning" (Ray Charles, Harry Nilsson), "Keep A-Knockin'" (Little Richard), "Caldonia" (Muddy Waters, B.B. King)

Louis Thomas Jordan was a jump blues innovator whose highly percussive, earthy alliterative phrasing is one of the earliest examples of proto-rap.

In 1936 he joined the Savoy Ballroom orchestra in New York City under bandleader Chick Webb; Ella Fitzgerald was their young female singer. Two years later, Jordan formed the Tympany Five and took up residence at Harlem's Elks Rendezvous.

In 1941 Jordan was paid union scale (thirty-five dollars per week for Louis; thirty-five dollars for the band); by 1948 he was grossing more than thirty-five thousand dollars per week. He produced "Knock Me a Kiss" (a 1942 cover hit for Roy Eldridge) and his own first hit, "I'm Gonna Move to the Outskirts of Town." His "answer record," "I'm Gonna Leave You on the Outskirts of Town," hit No. 2 on Billboard's Harlem Hit Parade. His next single, "What's the Use of Getting Sober (When You're Gonna Get Drunk Again)," hit No. 1. Jordan made "soundies" (music video ancestors) in Los Angeles. Armed Forces Radio appearances won him a mixed audience. His first crossover hit, 1943's "Ration Blues," spent six weeks at No. 1 and twenty-one weeks in the Top 10; 1944's "G.I. Jive"/"Is You Is or Is You Ain't My Baby?" crossed over to hit No. 1, sparked by Jordan's appearance in Universal's film *Follow the Boys.*

Jordan's "Saturday Night Fish Fry" (1950), with the word "rocking" in the chorus, makes it a contender for the first rock 'n' roll record. From 1942 to 1951, his popularity as a black bandleader nearly equaled Duke Ellington's and Count Basie's. "The King of the Jukebox," Jordan scored a record fifty-seven R&B chart hits. His commercial decline began in the 1950s, despite making many fine recordings. Lounge gigs gave him a steady income until he succumbed to a heart attack.

TRIVIA: Billboard's fifth all-time most successful black recording artist, Jordan is the top black recording artist of all time in terms of total number of weeks in the No. 1 spot: 113. (Stevie Wonder is second with 70.) Louis popularized the term "chick" to refer to a woman.

LOUIS JORDAN

ALBERT KING

(ALBERT NELSON)

MAIN INSTRUMENTS: Guitar, vocals
BORN: Indianola, Mississippi; April 25, 1923
DIED: Memphis, Tennessee; December 21, 1992

RECOMMENDED TRACKS: "Born Under a Bad Sign," "Crosscut Saw," "The Hunter," "Laundromat Blues," "As the Years Go Passing By," "I'll Play the Blues for You"

INTERESTING COVERS: "Born Under a Bad Sign" (Cream), "Crosscut Saw" (Groundhogs), "The Hunter" (Free), "Laundromat Blues" (Rory Gallagher), "As the Years Go Passing By" (Eric Burdon and the Animals)

Raised in Forrest City, Arkansas, Albert created his first guitar from a cigar box. He played with gospel groups until he heard Lonnie Johnson and Blind Lemon Jefferson. In 1950, he joined the In the Groove Boys, then became Jimmy Reed's drummer. B.B. King's "Three O'Clock Blues" inspired Albert to change his last name. Willie Dixon got him a 1953 audition at Parrot Records, then King rejoined the In the Groove Boys for two more years.

In 1956, Albert moved to St. Louis, where he quickly became a headliner. His first minor hit was Little Milton's "I'm a Lonely Man" in 1958. His first major hit was "Don't Throw Your Love on Me So Strong," which climbed to No. 14 on the R&B charts in 1961.

Albert signed to Stax in 1966. Backed by Booker T. and the MGs, he recorded the hits "Laundromat Blues" and "Crosscut Saw." *Born Under a Bad Sign*, an LP of his blues singles for Stax, won King huge crossover appeal. In 1969, he recorded three LPs, including his first true studio album, *Years Gone By*. In 1971 he used the Bar-Kays, the Memphis Horns, and the Movement to create a big, fat funk sound in contrast to his tough, spare MGs records. Their recordings included King's signature tune, "I'll Play the Blues for You."

In the mid-1970s, King left Stax for Utopia, Tomato, and Fantasy. He recorded two studio LPs for each of them, plus some live albums. Albert performed across America and Europe for the rest of the decade, until his sudden death from a heart attack.

TRIVIA: King was nicknamed "the Velvet Bulldozer." The southpaw usually played right-handed guitars (like his Gibson Flying V "Lucy") flipped over so his low E was on the bottom. He pulled down on the strings—instead of pushing up, like most players—giving him his unique tone. Eric Clapton said King inspired "Strange Brew," which uses Albert's "Personal Manager" solo.

FRIDAY 13

ALBERT KING

B.B. KING

(RILEY B. KING)

MAIN INSTRUMENTS: Guitar, vocals
BORN: Itta Bena, Mississippi; September 16, 1925

RECOMMENDED TRACKS: The entire *Live at the Regal* LP, "When My Heart Beats Like a Hammer," "Bad Luck," "Sweet Sixteen," "Partin' Time"

INTERESTING COVERS: "Sweet Little Angel" (Jeff Beck Group), "When My Heart Beats Like a Hammer" (Fleetwood Mac)

INTERESTING COLLABORATION: "When Love Comes to Town" (with U2)

His father deserted his family when Riley B. King was four. He was sent to his maternal grandmother to be raised. He worked as a sharecropper and sang gospel. Country music also influenced him, as did Charlie Christian, Lonnie Johnson, and Django Reinhardt. King moved to Indianola, Mississippi, then studied guitar in Memphis under his cousin Bukka White. After months of hardship, he returned to Indianola.

By 1948 King was back in Memphis, working as a singer and disc jockey and gaining the nickname "Beale Street Blues Boy" (shortened to "B.B."). Upon hearing T-Bone Walker, King purchased an electric guitar. King's first R&B No. 1 was Lowell Fulson's "Three O'Clock Blues," cut at a YMCA in 1951.

B.B. was performing at an Arkansas dance in the mid-1950s when a kerosene heater got knocked over during a fight and set the place on fire. He evacuated with the crowd, then realized his beloved thirty-dollar acoustic guitar was still inside. He dashed back to retrieve it, narrowly escaping death. He learned that the brawl was over a woman named Lucille, so he named his guitar "Lucille" as a reminder never to be so crazy as to fight over a woman. Since then, each of his Gibsons has been named Lucille. The original Lucille was stolen from his car trunk in Brooklyn. He offered a huge reward, but no one ever came forward. He says today he would give a hundred thousand dollars for that guitar.

King's majestic *Live at the Regal* LP in 1964 captured an enormous late-1960s blues revival crossover audience. His 1969 Grammy winner, "The Thrill Is Gone," was a huge pop and R&B hit. Between 1951 and 1985, King scored seventy-four times on the R&B charts.

B.B. King gigged three hundred nights a year in the 1980s and '90s and he still performs worldwide. The B.B. King Museum opened in 2008.

TRIVIA: Boxer Sonny Liston was B.B.'s uncle. King is a vegetarian, a licensed pilot, and a nondrinker and nonsmoker. B.B.'s favorite singer is Frank Sinatra.

B.B. KING

LEAD BELLY

(HUDDIE WILLIAM LEDBETTER)

MAIN INSTRUMENTS: Vocals, twelve-string guitar,
accordion, piano, mandolin, violin
BORN: Mooringsport, Louisiana; January 23 (?), 1888
DIED: New York, New York; December 6, 1949

RECOMMENDED TRACKS: "Black Betty," "Gallis Pole," "Boll Weevil," "New Orleans (Rising Sun Blues)," "Where Did You Sleep Last Night?" "The Bourgeois Blues"

INTERESTING COVERS: "Black Betty" (Manfred Mann as "Big Betty"), "Gallis Pole" (Led Zeppelin as "Gallows Pole"), "Midnight Special" (Creedence Clearwater Revival), "Boll Weevil" (White Stripes), "New Orleans" (Animals as "House of the Rising Sun"), "Where Did You Sleep Last Night?" (Long John Baldry as "Black Girl"), "The Bourgeois Blues" (Rolling Stones as "When the Whip Comes Down")

Born Huddie Ledbetter, Lead Belly's prison moniker was a play on his last name, his toughness, or his capacity for homemade liquor—or maybe his having been gut shot with buckshot.

Ledbetter's uncle gave him his first instrument, an accordion, and as a teen the plantation-born singer played Shreveport's red-light district. Huddie was known for his superior twelve-string guitar abilities and his vast songbook of folk standards; he teamed for years with Blind Lemon Jefferson.

In 1915 Lead Belly worked a chain gang for "carrying a pistol." He escaped but was returned for killing a relative over a woman. He was pardoned after he wrote a song appealing to the governor (paroles were unheard of back then in the South). In 1930, he served four more years in prison for knifing a white man. John and Alan Lomax recorded hundreds of his songs for the Library of Congress during a prison visit. Lead Belly gained early release for good behavior, after which John Lomax took him on as a driver. *Time* magazine made one of its first newsreels about "the convict who sang his way out of prison."

He married in 1935 and after a college lecture tour, John Lomax soured on Lead Belly and sent the couple packing. He sued Lomax for his recording money, and severed management ties. Lead Belly hit with concerts for leftist folk music fans. After Alan Lomax raised money for Lead Belly's defense for a 1939 assault, he was a regular on Alan's radio show. The first country blues musician to see success in Europe, he fell ill with Lou Gehrig's disease on his first tour. His final concert was a memorial tribute to John Lomax.

TRIVIA: Bob Dylan remarked that Lead Belly was "one of the few ex-cons who recorded a popular children's album [*Lead Belly Sings For Children*]."

HUDDIE
"LEAD BELLY" LEDBETTER

J. B. LENOIR

MAIN INSTRUMENTS: Guitar, vocals
BORN: Monticello, Mississippi; March 5, 1929
DIED: Urbana, Illinois; April 29, 1967

RECOMMENDED TRACKS: "Let's Roll," "The Mojo," "Eisenhower Blues," "Mamma Talk to Your Daughter," "Don't Dog Your Woman," "Don't Touch My Head"

Lenoir's guitarist father introduced him to Blind Lemon Jefferson's songs; Arthur Crudup and Lightnin' Hopkins were other early influences. During the 1940s Lenoir worked with Sonny Boy Williamson II and Elmore James in New Orleans.

Lenoir moved to Chicago in 1949, and Big Bill Broonzy connected him with the local blues scene. There, he would he perform with Memphis Minnie, Muddy Waters, and Big Maceo.

His first Chess Records single was 1951's topical "Korea Blues." He recorded for J.O.B. Records with Sunnyland Slim and others through 1953. "Eisenhower Blues" caused a backlash, so Parrot Records pulled the song, rereleasing it as "Tax Paying Blues."

Lenoir's 1954 and 1955 Parrot and 1955 to 1958 Checker catalogs all boast fine J. B. selections. His 1963 band, J. B. Lenoir and His African Hunch Rhythm, represented his interest in African percussion. Then gigs dried up, and he worked in a university kitchen in Champaign, where he was found by Willie Dixon. Dixon produced his political LPs *Alabama Blues* (1965) and *Down in Mississippi* (1966), with songs expressing the social concerns raised by the 1960s civil rights and free speech protests. In 1965 Lenoir toured Europe and performed with the American Folk Blues Festival in England.

He died from a heart attack related to injuries he received three weeks earlier in an auto accident.

Lenoir was always known by the initials J. B. He was famed for his showy performances, high-register vocals, and faux-zebra skin coats. He was an influential guitar player and composer. The strong, politically charged commentary of his lyrics set him apart from other bluesmen.

TRIVIA: John Mayall mourned Lenoir's passing in two songs: "I'm Gonna Fight for You, J. B." and "Death of J. B. Lenoir."

J.B. LENOIR

MEADE LUX LEWIS

MAIN INSTRUMENT: Piano
BORN: Chicago, Illinois; September 3 (or 4 or 13), 1905
DIED: Minneapolis, Minnesota; June 7, 1964

RECOMMENDED TRACKS: "Honky Tonk Train Blues," "Boogie Woogie Prayer," "Six Wheel Chaser," "Bass on Top," "Mr. Freddie Blues," "Frompy Stomp"

INTERESTING COVERS: "Honky Tonk Train Blues" (Keith Emerson, Bob Zurke with Bob Crosby, George Wright with drummer Cozy Cole as "Organ Boogie")

Meade Anderson Lewis grew up under the spell of pianist Jimmy Yancey. Lux played frequently in late-1920s Chicago. He debuted on record in 1927 with "Honky Tonk Train Blues" for Paramount. It was so popular that he rerecorded it for Parlaphone in 1935 and for Victor in 1937. This blues piano classic was heavily covered by other musicians as well. John Hammond searched for Lewis after hearing it in 1935 and discovered him working at a Chicago carwash. The following year, Lewis became the first jazz pianist/jazz celeste player (he added a little harpsichord as well in 1941). Lux's Carnegie Hall performance at Hammond's historic 1938 *From Spirituals to Swing* event brought him great acclaim. After the concert, Lewis formed the Boogie Woogie Trio with Albert Ammons and Pete Johnson, both of whom had also performed at the show. The three greatest boogie pianists of their day, they scored a long booking at Café Society and toured together, launching a national ten-year boogie-woogie mania.

Record producer Alfred Lion was so taken with the Carnegie Hall performances of Lewis and Ammons that two weeks later he created the now-famous jazz label Blue Note Records and made *Albert Ammons and Meade Lux Lewis: The First Day* Blue Note's first recording. Lewis led sessions for most of the major record companies after that.

After his star and the boogie craze faded, Lewis found gigs in California and Chicago. He struggled against his boogie-woogie and blues typecasting and spent the rest of his life performing ragtime numbers and Tin Pan Alley pop standards in response. Lux died in a car crash.

TRIVIA: Lewis appeared, uncredited, in the movie classic *It's a Wonderful Life*, pounding the eighty-eights in the scene where Nick tosses George Bailey out of his bar. He also appeared in the movies *New Orleans* (1947) and *Nightmare* (1956).

MEADE LUX LEWIS

SMILEY LEWIS

(OVERTON AMOS LEMONS)

MAIN INSTRUMENT: Vocals
BORN: DeQuincy, Louisiana; July 5, 1913
DIED: New Orleans, Louisiana; October 7, 1966

RECOMMENDED TRACKS: "I Hear You Knocking," "Shame, Shame, Shame," "Blue Monday," "One Night"

INTERESTING COVERS: "I Hear You Knocking" (Dave Edmunds, Gale Storm), "Shame, Shame, Shame" (Merseybeats, Aerosmith), "Blue Monday" (Fats Domino, Dave Edmunds), "One Night" (Elvis Presley)

Overton Lemons's mother died while he was a boy. In his teens, he hopped a freight train but then couldn't get off until its first stop: New Orleans. He adopted the last name of the white family who kindly took him in.

Lewis began playing French Quarter clubs and bars in the Seventh Ward as "Smiling Lewis," a name referencing his missing front teeth. He often sang with pianist Tuts Washington when they were both in Thomas Jefferson's Dixieland band in the mid-1930s. When the band broke up, Lewis played clubs for tips. Smiley married in 1938; they lived with his wife's mother.

Lewis labored by day and sang by night. During WWII, he rejoined Tuts in "Kid" Mollier's band. They played for Fort Polk soldiers and became the Boogie Woogie Club's house band. As a trio after the war, they returned to the French Quarter. DeLuxe Records recorded Lewis's debut album, *Here Comes Smiley*, in 1947. Despite "Turn On Your Volume Baby" hitting locally, DeLuxe never asked him back and left the other songs he had in the can unreleased.

Producer Dave Bartholomew invited the trio to an Imperial session, resulting in the New Orleans staple "Tee-Nah-Nah." Smiley's first national charter was 1952's "The Bells Are Ringing." Nineteen fifty-four produced "Blue Monday," later a hit for Fats Domino. His biggest smash was his recording of Bartholomew's "I Hear You Knocking," a 1955 No. 2 R&B hit and a hit once again for Welsh rocker Dave Edmunds in 1971 (No. 4 in the U.S., No. 1 in the U.K.). "One Night (of Sin)" made the R&B top twenty in 1956. Elvis Presley's sanitized version hit No. 4 nationally in 1958.

In 1957 Imperial had Smiley record pop and country music. The idea bombed, and Lewis was let go. In the early 1960s he arrived at New Orleans gigs via the city bus. In 1965, a suspected ulcer turned out to be stomach cancer. Bartholomew quickly put together a benefit show, but it was too late. Smiley died in the arms of his second wife three days before the show.

SMILEY LEWIS

LIGHTNIN' SLIM

(OTIS V. HICKS)

MAIN INSTRUMENTS: Guitar, vocals
BORN: St. Louis, Missouri; March 13, 1913
DIED: Detroit, Michigan; July 27, 1974

RECOMMENDED TRACKS: "Rooster Blues," "I'm Evil," "Somebody Knockin'"

After living on a farm outside of St. Louis, Missouri, the Hicks family moved to St. Francisville, Louisiana, when Slim was thirteen. He was taught guitar basics by his father and older brother. By 1946, Slim was playing Baton Rouge bars, first with Big Poppa's band, then on his own. He worked his way up to club dates and radio broadcasts in the 1950s.

Slim's single debut was 1954's "Bad Luck" ("If it wasn't for bad luck, I wouldn't have no luck at all") on Feature Records. He recorded regional hits for Excello Records for twelve years, often partnering with his brother-in-law Slim Harpo and harmonica ace Lazy Lester. In 1960 "Rooster Blues" made the national R&B charts. His first Excello LP was released the following year. He then left music and ended up working at either a steam laundry or a foundry in Pontiac, Michigan, during the 1960s. Whichever is correct, his hands suffered from the constant exposure to extremely high temperatures.

In 1970, a fan found Lightnin' Slim in a little Pontiac room rented from Slim Harpo's sister. The fan helped him begin performing again and arranged for a new Excello contract. His comeback show was a 1971 reunion with Lazy Lester at the University of Chicago Folk Festival. He toured Europe in the early 1970s, playing to appreciative blues audiences at events like the Montreux Jazz Festival, and performed at American festivals and hippie concerts with Slim Harpo. Harpo's sudden death took Slim by surprise. He soldiered on alone, dying a few years later of stomach cancer in Detroit.

Lightnin' Slim was an important force in the Louisiana and swamp blues music worlds. He regularly transformed other musicians' material with his own sadly weary, seen-it-all style. Fans and associates remember Slim as a stylish man who sported flashy suits and an infectious sense of humor.

TRIVIA: His oft-recorded call before the instrumental break, "Blow your harmonica, son," has become one of the most enduring catchphrases of the blues.

LIGHTNIN' SLIM

LITTLE WALTER

(MARION WALTER JACOBS)

MAIN INSTRUMENTS: Harmonica, vocals, guitar
BORN: Marksville, Louisiana; May 1, 1930
DIED: Chicago, Illinois; February 15, 1968

RECOMMENDED TRACKS: "Blues with a Feeling," "My Babe," "Mellow Down Easy,"
"Roller Coaster," "Juke," "Boom Boom Out Go the Lights," "Off the Wall," "Teenage Beat"

INTERESTING COVERS: "My Babe" (Tom Jones), "Off the Wall" (Paul Butterfield Blues
Band), "Blues with a Feeling" (Paul Butterfield Blues Band), "Boom Boom Out Go
the Lights" (J. Geils Band)

Walter was raised in Rapides Parish, Louisiana, and quit school at age twelve. He played and sang on the streets of New Orleans, Memphis, Helena, and St. Louis. He picked up his musical chops on guitar and harp chops from Sonny Boy Williamson II, Sunnyland Slim, and Honeyboy Edwards, then hit Chicago in 1945 and began recording. He snagged some guitar sessions work but quickly became better known for his harmonica work. Unable to be heard over electric guitarists, Little Walter cupped his hands around his harp and a small microphone, turned up the volume and let loose, transforming that little instrument forever. He was not the first to amplify the blues harp (that might have been Big Walter Horton), but he was the first harmonica player to intentionally use electronic distortion to his advantage.

The teen prodigy joined Tampa Red and Big Bill Broonzy on the thriving Maxwell Street scene. Walter's record debut was in 1947 on Ora-Nelle. He became an important part of Muddy Waters's band in 1948 and recorded as a guitarist with Muddy, Baby Face Leroy Foster, and Jimmy Rogers.

Little Walter's own career took off when he signed with Chess subsidiary Checker in 1952. "Juke" spent eight weeks at No. 1 on Billboard's R&B charts—the only harmonica instrumental ever to do so, and Chess's biggest hit up until then. He scored fourteen Top 10 R&B hits between 1952 and 1958, including the No. 1 "My Babe" in 1955. Hard drinking and a nasty temper hastened his steep decline. After returning from a second European tour, he got into a fight at a South Side Chicago club. Although the brawl's damage was minor, his new injuries exacerbated those from previous scrapes. He died in his sleep at his girlfriend's apartment the next morning.

Walter's influence shows in nearly every subsequent blues harpist. He is the only musician in the Rock and Roll Hall of Fame solely for his work as a harmonica player.

LITTLE WALTER

LONESOME SUNDOWN

(CORNELIUS GREEN)

MAIN INSTRUMENTS: Guitar, vocals
BORN: Dugas Plantation (near Donaldsonville), Louisiana; December 12, 1928
DIED: Gonzales, Louisiana; April 23, 1995

RECOMMENDED TRACKS: "My Home Is a Prison," "My Home Ain't Here," "I Stood By," "Don't Say a Word," "You Know I Love You," "Gonna Stick to You Baby"

At eighteen, Cornelius Green moved to New Orleans, where he took whatever jobs came his way. Muddy Waters and John Lee Hooker inspired him to return home and learn guitar from a cousin. After working as a trucker, Green moved to Port Arthur, Texas, in 1953 for work at the Gulf Oil refinery. Zydeco legend Clifton Chenier saw him jamming; invited him to sit in with his band, the Zydeco Ramblers; and then hired Green as his guitarist. His Chenier tour included Chicago and Los Angeles, where Green's snoozing during a session inspired Chenier's "The Cat's Dreaming."

Green married in 1955, left Chenier, moved to Opelousas, Louisiana, and began composing his own songs. A demo tape inspired Jay Miller to produce Green and rename him Lonesome Sundown. In 1956, they leased their first collaboration, "Leave My Money Alone," to Excello Records. It sold okay, but their follow-up, "Lonesome Whistler," did even better. As part of Miller's stable, Sundown never charted, but he had eight years of healthy sales.

Miller described Lonesome's somber, down-home blues as "the sound of the swamp." By 1965 Sundown had many aching swamp classics under his belt, but had become disillusioned by his lack of success. After a devastating divorce, he left the music biz. Sundown worked as a laborer and became a minister at the Lord Jesus Christ of the Apostolic Faith Fellowship Throughout the World Church. He was coaxed into making the 1977 LP *Been Gone Too Long*, a superb comeback that, unfortunately, didn't sell. His final single from the LP was "I Betcha."

After playing the 1979 New Orleans Jazz and Heritage Festival and touring Sweden and Japan, Lonesome Sundown left the music industry for good. A year before he died, Sundown had a stroke that, sadly and ironically, robbed him of his ability to speak.

LONESOME SUNDOWN

WILLIE MABON

(WILLIAM JAMES MABON)

MAIN INSTRUMENTS: Vocals, piano
BORN: Hollywood, Tennessee; October 24, 1925
DIED: Paris, France; April 19, 1985

RECOMMENDED TRACKS: "I Don't Know," "Seventh Son," "I'm Mad," "Poison Ivy," "Got to Have Some," "The Fixer"

INTERESTING COVERS: "Seventh Son" (Johnny Rivers, Mose Allison, Climax Blues Band), "I Don't Know" (Blues Brothers), "Just Got Some" (Rod Stewart)

Raised in Memphis, Tennessee, Willie Mabon was already a recognized singer and pianist before he moved to Chicago in 1942. He first recorded as Big Willie for Apollo Records in 1949 and as the Blues Rockers for Aristocrat (which evolved into Chess Records) and Chess in 1950, then under his own name for Chess after that. Mabon's style was unique within the Chess stable; jazzy and suave, it spotlighted sax and piano instead of guitar and harmonica.

In 1952, "I Don't Know," a Mabon cover of a novelty song by boogie-woogie pianist Cripple Clarence Lofton, stayed at No. 1 on the Billboard R&B charts for eight weeks. It was Chess's greatest hit prior to those by Chuck Berry and Bo Diddley, Mabon's biggest career success, and one of the first R&B hits to be covered by a top white performer (Tennessee Ernie Ford). Alan Freed played Mabon's version on his radio show, exposing white teens to it and expanding the early rock 'n' roll crossover market.

Mabon hit No. 1 again with 1953's "I'm Mad" and then scored with "Poison Ivy" in 1954. The rest of his Chess output didn't chart. He had regional hits with other labels, but his career never regained its steam after he left Chess.

Many health issues began to surface in the late 1960s. He moved to Paris in 1972, played at the 1973 Montreux Jazz Festival, and, despite a long illness, recorded and toured all over Europe up until his death.

TRIVIA: Although Mabon's 1955 Chess version of Willie Dixon's hoodoo braggadocio "Seventh Son" missed, Johnny Rivers's cover version hit No. 7 nationally in 1965. English R&B singer-keyboardist Georgie Fame was greatly influenced by Mabon's wry, cool, and casual style. Willie's "I'm Mad" is featured in *Sing Beast Sing*, a 1980 Marv Newland cartoon short.

SARA MARTIN

(A.K.A. MARGARET JOHNSON, SALLY ROBERTS)

MAIN INSTRUMENT: Vocals
BORN: Louisville, Kentucky; June 18, 1884
DIED: Louisville, Kentucky; May 24, 1955

RECOMMENDED TRACKS: "T'aint Nobody's Bizness If I Do," "Mean Tight Mama,"
"Death Sting Me Blues," "Brother Ben"

INTERESTING COVERS: "T'aint Nobody's Bizness If I Do" (B.B. King, Billie Holiday,
Bessie Smith, Sam Cooke, Jimmy Witherspoon, Dinah Washington, Otis Spann)

Sara Martin began her career as a touring vaudeville singer, then switched to blues singing in the early 1920s. In 1922 she cut a number of ribald blues numbers for OKeh Records. Billed as "the Famous Moanin' Mama," "the Blues Sensation of the West," and "the Colored Sophie Tucker," she rose to become one of the most recorded and in-demand classic female blues singers of her time.

Sometimes recording as Margaret Johnson or Sally Roberts, Martin built her popularity on the southern Theater Owners Booking Association circuits, working up to playing clubs and then theaters on the East Coast. Sara toured and recorded through 1928, being backed at times by Fats Waller, Clarence Williams, King Oliver, and Sylvester Weaver. Accompanied by Waller on piano in 1922, she appears to have been the first to record the blues standard "T'aint Nobody's Bizness If I Do."

Martin worked the late-1920s stages of New York, Detroit, Pittsburgh, and the Caribbean, ending her stage career with Darktown Scandals Review in 1930. She performed with gospel legend and former bluesman Thomas "Georgia Tom" Dorsey in 1932, then left the music business and returned to her hometown of Louisville. She managed a nursing home and, on occasion, sang gospel in church. Martin died after a stroke.

TRIVIA: Sara Martin was known for her grand onstage performing style and extravagant multiple costume changes. She appeared in one film, *Hello Bill* (1929), with Bill "Bojangles" Robinson.

SARA MARTIN

PERCY MAYFIELD

MAIN INSTRUMENT: Vocals
BORN: Minden, Louisiana; August 12, 1920
DIED: Los Angeles, California; August 11, 1984

RECOMMENDED TRACKS: "Hit the Road Jack," "Please Send Me Someone to Love," "Strange Things Happening," "Lost Love," "Cry Baby," "Big Question"

INTERESTING COVERS: "Hit the Road Jack" (Ray Charles, Animals, Easybeats), "At the Club" (Ray Charles), "Please Send Me Someone to Love" (Etta James)

Percy Mayfield's youthful knack for poetry led him to songwriting and singing. He first performed in his early twenties in Texas, and then in Los Angeles (1942), without success. Mayfield wrote "Two Years of Torture" with Jimmy Witherspoon in mind and submitted it to Supreme Records. Percy's demo so impressed Supreme that they pressed him to record it. A long, steady seller, the record caught the attention of Specialty Records, which signed him in 1950. He hit with several R&B tunes over the next few years, establishing his reputation as a fine blues balladeer.

Though Mayfield's smooth vocals were influenced by singers like Charles Brown, he didn't concentrate on crossing over to the white market like his fellow West Coast bluesmen did; he really just wrote to satisfy himself. Percy's quietly revealing, downbeat lyrics were echoed in his tempos. His 1950 R&B No. 1, "Please Send Me Someone to Love," became his most covered song. Percy's deep, dark pathos and aching vulnerability were masterfully communicated in songs like "Life Is Suicide" and "The River's Invitation."

In 1952, at the peak of his career, Mayfield's once-handsome face was brutally disfigured in a car wreck. It weakened his confidence and limited his performing, but never slowed this poet of the blues' prolific composing. He continued to write and record for Specialty, Chess, and Imperial, where he flourished.

In 1961, his song "Hit the Road Jack" caught the notice of Ray Charles, who signed Percy to Charles's own label, Tangerine Records. Mayfield continued to record, although his work for Tangerine was chiefly as a songwriter. Mayfield wrote and recorded into the 1970s with minor success while sporadically performing. By the time he died of a heart attack, he had faded from public consciousness.

TRIVIA: Percy's only studio recording of his best-known song, "Hit the Road Jack," is just a very casual demo, basically an a cappella duet. Mayfield died the day before his birthday.

PERCY MAYFIELD

PAPA CHARLIE McCOY

(CHARLES McCOY)

MAIN INSTRUMENTS: Guitar, mandolin
BORN: Jackson, Mississippi; May 26, 1909
DIED: Chicago, Illinois; July 26, 1950

RECOMMENDED TRACKS: "The Vicksburg Stomp," "Too Long," "Keep on Trying"

INTERESTING COVERS: "Baltimore Blues" (Robert Johnson as "Sweet Home Chicago"), "Too Long" (Bob Dunn's Vagabonds), "The Vicksburg Stomp" (Mike Compton)

With older brother Kansas Joe McCoy, self-taught musician Papa Charlie McCoy was one of the major blues sidemen of his era. His deft, thoughtful guitar playing enhanced the recordings of many artists.

Charlie played guitar and mandolin with his band, the Mississippi Hot Footers, throughout the Delta. By the late 1920s he was recording on a frequent basis. He provided live and session backing for the Mississippi Sheiks, Rubin Lacy, and many other Delta bluesmen whose touring led them through Jackson. As a slide guitarist, he recorded as Tampa Kid.

McCoy's recordings with Bo Carter (as the Mississippi Mud Steppers) included two versions of Cow Cow Davenport's "Cow Cow Blues." The instrumental arrangement was retitled "The Jackson Stomp"; McCoy wrote new lyrics for the other version, which he sang, renaming it "The Lonesome Train That Took My Girl from Town."

Charlie also performed and recorded for years with his brother Joe as the McCoy Brothers. With his warm, high vocals, Charlie could have been a headliner; he just seemed to prefer a supporting role. His own "Baltimore Blues" is the first recorded version of the blues classic later known as "Sweet Home Chicago."

McCoy moved to Chicago in the mid-1930s, and formed Papa Charlie's Boys and was an original member of Harlem Hamfats, a band that included his brother Joe. Charlie's WWII service resulted in poor health that prematurely ended his career. His last recording was done in 1942. Charlie died from paralytic brain disease just months after Joe passed from heart disease.

As is often the case with blues musicians of their era, the McCoy Brothers' gravesites went unmarked for decades. A 2010 benefit concert raised enough funds to purchase gravestones for both of these gentlemen of the blues.

TRIVIA: Papa Charlie McCoy was the brother-in-law of Memphis Minnie (1897–1973). He played mandolin on some of Minnie's mid-1930s sessions.

PAPA CHARLIE McCOY

KANSAS JOE McCOY

(JOE McCOY)

MAIN INSTRUMENT: Guitar
BORN: Raymond, Mississippi; May 11, 1905
DIED: Chicago, Illinois; January 28, 1950

RECOMMENDED TRACKS: "Bumble Bee" (with Memphis Minnie), "When the Levee Breaks" (with Memphis Minnie)

INTERESTING COVERS: "When the Levee Breaks" (Led Zeppelin, Bob Dylan), "Why Don't You Do Right?" (Lil Green, Peggy Lee, Benny Goodman)

Joe McCoy had many aliases (Bill Wither, Georgio Pine Boy, Hallelujah Joe, the Mississippi Mudder, Hillbilly Plowboy, Mud Dauber Joe, and Hamfoot Ham), but it was Kansas Joe McCoy that stuck, despite his not being from Kansas. His older brother, Papa Charlie McCoy, and Joe were two of the greatest blues sidemen of their era. A self-taught guitarist, Joe was attracted to the mid-1920s Memphis, Tennessee, music scene. He joined Jed Davenport's Beale Street Jug Band and then teamed with Lizzie Douglas (a.k.a. Memphis Minnie), becoming her second husband. Joe's spare, elegant slide style is well captured on the landmark recordings he made with Minnie.

Joe and Minnie hit in 1929 with "Bumble Bee" on Columbia. In 1930 the couple moved to Chicago, where they, Big Bill Broonzy, and Tampa Red led the forefront of modernizing and urbanizing country blues. After Joe and Minnie ended their six-year marriage, he and Charlie became original members of Harlem Hamfats (none of whom were from New York, much less Harlem), which recorded from 1936 to 1939. In 1941 Joe revamped a 1936 Hamfats song, "The Weed Smoker's Dream," as "Why Don't You Do Right?" for Lil Green. Peggy Lee covered it (it was her first hit) and it became Joe's most timeless composition.

At the onset of WWII, the Army grabbed Charlie, but Joe's heart condition left him at home. He put together Big Joe and His Washboard Band (later, Big Joe and His Rhythm) during the mid-1940s. The latter version of the band, which included Charlie on mandolin and Robert Nighthawk on harp, performed throughout the 1940s. Joe died of heart disease just months prior to his brother Charlie's death.

In 1971, Robert Plant shared Memphis Minnie's "When the Levee Breaks" with Jimmy Page. They rearranged it, changed some of the lyrics, and recorded it for *Led Zeppelin IV*. John Mellencamp, the Ink Spots, Ella Fitzgerald, and Jo Ann Kelly have also covered Joe's songs.

Joe could have been a star on his own, but, like Charlie, he seemed happier in a musical background role.

KANSAS JOE McCOY

JIMMY McCRACKLIN

(JAMES DAVID WALKER)

MAIN INSTRUMENTS: Vocals, piano
BORN: St. Louis, Missouri; August 13, 1921

RECOMMENDED TRACKS: "The Walk," "Tramp" (recorded by cowriter Lowell Fulson), "Georgia Slop," "Every Night, Every Day," "Shame, Shame, Shame"

INTERESTING COVERS: "The Walk" (Inmates), "Tramp" (Otis Redding and Carla Thomas, Julie Driscoll and the Brian Auger Trinity, Buddy Guy, ZZ Top), "Georgia Slop" (Big Al Downing), "Every Night, Every Day" (Magic Sam)

Jimmy McCracklin was taught piano by his pa's acquaintance, Walter Davis. After WWII naval service, McCracklin left St. Louis for Richmond, California, and made his recording debut in 1945. He formed a group called Jimmy McCracklin and His Blues Blasters in 1946. They became the house band at his sister-in-law's Club Savoy, often supporting musicians such as B.B. King and Charles Brown.

McCracklin recorded for several small Los Angeles and Oakland labels before signing with Modern (1949–1950), Swing Time (1951), and then Peacock (1952–1954). He returned to Modern in 1954 with a hot, new sax-driven sound.

Sessions for the indie label Irma (later released on Imperial) were followed by McCracklin's 1958 guest spot on *American Bandstand* on which he performed his simple but powerful instrumental "The Walk." Checker Records rush-released it and the song became Jimmy's breakout Top 10 hit. "The Walk" had a great musical hook that popped up later in Freddie King's "Hideaway." After more singles, Jimmy left Checker for Mercury, where he cut 1959's rockin' "Georgia Slop." "Just Got to Know" was a 1961 R&B No. 2 hit for his own Oakland Art-Tone label. Chess released McCracklin's first solo LP of West Coast blues, *Jimmy McCracklin Sings*, in 1962. His unyielding "Think" hit in 1965.

Jimmy wrote "Tramp" for guitarist Lowell Fulson. Months after Fulson's release, "Tramp" became a 1967 hit for Otis Redding and Carla Thomas on Stax Records. McCracklin then joined Stax himself, cutting three LPs for them in the 1970s.

Jimmy recorded new albums in the 1980s and '90s and toured clubs and blues festivals. He is still performing, recording, and acting like a much younger man.

TRIVIA: By his own count, McCracklin has written nearly a thousand songs. Bob Dylan has named Jimmy as a favorite. The Southern California group The Blasters named themselves after McCracklin's backup band.

JIMMY McCRACKLIN

MISSISSIPPI FRED McDOWELL

MAIN INSTRUMENTS: Vocals, guitar
BORN: Rossville, Tennessee; January 12, 1904
DIED: Memphis, Tennessee; July 3, 1972

RECOMMENDED TRACKS: "You Gotta Move," "Baby Please Don't Go," "Good Morning Little School Girl," "Jesus Is on the Mainline"

INTERESTING COVERS: "You Gotta Move" (Rolling Stones), "Write Me a Few Lines" (Bonnie Raitt), "Kokomo" (Bonnie Raitt)

Orphan Fred McDowell began playing guitar at Rossville, Tennessee, dances at age fourteen using a pocketknife for a slide, a hollowed-out steer bone slide, and then a glass slide (for its clearer sound). In 1926 he played for tips on the streets of Memphis. Despite the fact that he was Tennessee-born, Fred never minded his "Mississippi" moniker, since he ultimately settled in Como, Mississippi, in 1940 and spent the rest of his life there. He divided his time between farming and music, playing weekends at area fish fries, picnics, and house parties.

This lifestyle remained unchanged for thirty years, until he was "discovered" in 1959 by folklorist Alan Lomax, who recorded him for Atlantic's American folk music series. Fred continued farming and playing for tips until Arhoolie Records chief Chris Strachwitz located him in 1964 and recorded two LPs, *Fred McDowell* (*Volume 1* and *2*), that stunned folk-blues fans. These records and the 1960s folk/blues revival made McDowell's career take off with gigs aplenty, including the Newport Folk Festival, coffeehouses throughout the United States, and the American Folk Blues Festival in Europe.

While he famously declared "I do not play no rock and roll" (his 1969 Capitol LP, *I Do Not Play No Rock 'n' Roll*, was his first on electric guitar), Fred liked hanging with young rockers like Bonnie Raitt, whom he personally tutored on her slide technique. His version of North Mississippi blues was close in structure to its African roots, often trading chord changes for a more hypnotic, single chord drone effect.

He appeared in the films *The Blues Maker* (1968), *Fred McDowell* (1969), and *Roots of American Music: Country and Urban Music* (1970). While still performing, he was diagnosed with cancer in 1971 and died the next year. Twenty years later, his barren gravesite received a memorial paid for by Bonnie Raitt.

TRIVIA: The Rolling Stones invited Fred to Europe and bought him a silver-lamé suit, which he wore home and was eventually buried in. The rich catalog of Delta blues that Fred drew from was recorded by players in the 1920s and early '30s.

MEMPHIS SLIM

(JOHN LEN CHATMAN, A.K.A. JOHN "PETER" CHATMAN)

MAIN INSTRUMENTS: Piano, vocals
BORN: Memphis, Tennessee; September 3, 1915
DIED: Paris, France; February 24, 1988

RECOMMENDED TRACKS: "Mother Earth," "Lend Me Your Love," "Rockin' the House," "Nobody Loves Me," "Messin' Around (With the Blues)"

INTERESTING COVERS: "Nobody Loves Me" (a.k.a. "Everyday I Have the Blues": B.B. King, Lowell Fulson, James Brown, Natalie Cole), "Mother Earth" (Mother Earth)

Memphis Slim played Arkansas and Missouri honky-tonks, gambling joints, and dance halls during the 1930s. In Chicago he paired with Big Bill Broonzy for club work. His Bluebird records were his first releases as "Memphis Slim" (so-named by producer Lester Melrose; he published his songs, though, as Peter Chatman). He supported Broonzy, Washboard Sam, Sonny Boy Williamson II, and Jazz Gillum as a Bluebird session man. He took Big Bill's advice about developing his own style instead of imitating his idol, Roosevelt Sykes, and in 1944 Slim emerged on his own. In a short time, Memphis Slim's thundering piano attack had its own imitators.

Post-WWII saw a blues-recording decline by the majors. Slim worked with small indies and recorded "Rockin' the House," from which his band the House Rockers got its name. His 1947 Miracle cut "Nobody Loves Me" became a blues standard as "Every Day I Have the Blues." Folklorist Alan Lomax recorded Slim, Broonzy, and Williamson in 1947 for the BBC documentary *The Art of the Negro* (expanded later as the LP *Blues in the Mississippi Night*). After Slim's 1948 R&B No. 1 "Messin' Around (With the Blues)," he toured. Miracle became Premium (for whom he recorded his classic "Mother Earth"). After that label's demise in 1951, Slim label-hopped for a while, then cut definitive versions of his best-known songs for his classic 1959 Vee-Jay LP *Memphis Slim at the Gate of the Horn*.

In 1960 Memphis Slim toured Europe with Willie Dixon, returning in 1962 in the first of the Dixon-organized American Folk Festival concerts. Slim chose to live in Paris for the last thirty years of his life, appearing on European TV, acting in French films (and scoring one), and performing throughout Europe and the United States. In his final years, Slim toured Europe with jazz drummer George Collier. After Collier's death in 1987, Slim rarely appeared in public. One of the greatest blues pianists ever, the prolific (with more than five hundred recordings) Mr. Chatman died of renal failure.

AMOS MILBURN

MAIN INSTRUMENTS: Vocals, piano
BORN: Houston, Texas; April 1, 1927
DIED: Houston, Texas; January 3, 1980

RECOMMENDED TRACKS: "Down the Road Apiece," "Chicken Shack Boogie," "One Scotch, One Bourbon, One Beer," "Bad, Bad Whiskey," "Hold Me Baby"

INTERESTING COVERS: "Down the Road Apiece" (Manfred Mann, Rolling Stones), "Chicken Shack Boogie" (Chicken Shack), "One Scotch, One Bourbon, One Beer" (George Thorogood and the Destroyers)

One of thirteen children, Amos Milburn was playing the piano at age five. As a teenager in the Navy he earned thirteen battle stars in the Philippines. Back in Houston he organized a sixteen-piece club band, becoming one of the first performers to switch from cool, urban jazz stylings to a more raucous jump-blues style, emphasizing rhythm over vocal and instrumental intricacies.

After his manager barged into the Aladdin Records boss's hospital room to play him a Milburn demo, Amos was signed in 1946. He sang velvety Charles Brown–like blues ballads (the two became friends) in addition to horn-driven boogies. He recorded more than seventy-five songs for Aladdin. "Chicken Shack Boogie" (1948) was the first of his nineteen Top 10 R&B hits. Milburn became a popular touring artist and a key Central Avenue player in black Los Angeles. He had several other booze-themed hits after his 1950 No. 1 "Bad, Bad Whiskey." Some claim alcoholism brought down the pianist; others swear Amos never had a liquor problem.

Milburn often appeared on the mid-1950s TV series *Showtime at the Apollo*. After a Midwest tour, he disbanded his combo, went solo, then joined Charles Brown for a Southern tour. He played one-nighters for three years before returning to Houston to reform his band. By then his string of hits had ended. After he left Aladdin in 1957, it closed its doors. His Ace efforts were unsuccessful.

Milburn recorded "Christmas (Comes But Once a Year)," the flip side of Charles Brown's "Please Come Home for Christmas" in 1960. Berry Gordy let Amos make a 1962 Motown LP (mostly remakes of his old hits), but nothing jump-started Amos's fading career. His final LP was in 1972 for Johnny Otis. Amos was so limited by a stroke that Otis had to play the left-hand piano parts. Amos lost his left leg from a second stroke, then died shortly after a third stroke.

TRIVIA: The English blues band Chicken Shack took its name from "Chicken Shack Boogie." In Houston, Amos Milburn was known as "the He-Man Martha Raye" before joining the Navy. Stevie Wonder played on Milburn's Motown LP.

AMOS MILBURN

LITTLE BROTHER MONTGOMERY

(EURREAL WILFORD MONTGOMERY)

MAIN INSTRUMENTS: Piano, vocals
BORN: Kentwood, Louisiana; April 18, 1906
DIED: Champaign, Illinois; September 6, 1985

RECOMMENDED TRACKS: "Shreveport Farewell," "Farrish Street Jive," "Vicksburg Blues," "No Special Rider," "First Time I Met the Blues"

INTERESTING COVER: "First Time I Met the Blues" (Buddy Guy)

Eurreal Montgomery was born in a sawmill town across Lake Pontchartrain from New Orleans, Louisiana. As a child he was "Little Brother Harper," as he resembled his father, Harper Montgomery, who owned a Louisiana barrelhouse. Eventually, the "Harper" got dropped. Little Brother played piano at age four; by eleven he'd given up school to play barrelhouses and juke joints. He also performed at Louisiana and Mississippi African American lumber and turpentine camps. He was influenced by Jelly Roll Morton, who used to visit the Montgomery family.

Little Brother first visited Chicago in the mid-1920s. His initial Paramount recordings, in 1930, included two signature tunes, "Vicksburg Blues" and "No Special Rider." In New Orleans from 1935 to 1936, Bluebird made even more recordings while Montgomery led a Jackson, Mississippi, swing band (1931–38). In 1942 Little Brother settled in Chicago, working blues and traditional jazz club gigs there in addition to touring Europe and America. He supported Otis Rush on several of his 1957 and 1958 Cobra dates. Buddy Guy's career got a big boost from recording Montgomery's "First Time I Met the Blues" (with Little Brother on piano) for Chess in 1960. Montgomery cut *Tasty Blues*, one of his finest LPs, for Bluesville in 1960.

In the late 1950s Little Brother was "discovered" by white audiences and tapped into the first wave of the folk-blues revival. Considered a living legend and serving as a prime Sunnyland Slim and Otis Spann influence, he was a link to the early blues and New Orleans music heydays. His fame grew even more during the 1960s blues boom. In 1969, Montgomery and his second wife launched their own record company, FM.

TRIVIA: "FM" came from "Floberg," his wife's maiden name, and "Montgomery," his own surname. In 1949 Little Brother played Carnegie Hall with Kid Ory's band. Little Brother played on two 1968 folk rock/pop LPs by Spanky and Our Gang.

LITTLE BROTHER MONTGOMERY

HAMBONE WILLIE NEWBERN

MAIN INSTRUMENTS: Guitar, vocals
BORN: Brownsville, Tennessee, area or eastern Arkansas (?); 1899
DIED: In an unknown prison; ca. 1947

RECOMMENDED TRACK: "Roll and Tumble Blues"

INTERESTING COVERS: "Roll and Tumble Blues" (as "Rollin' and Tumblin'": Muddy Waters, Cream, Canned Heat, Jeff Beck, Bob Dylan)

Reputed to have been born in 1899, Hambone Willie Newbern lived in the Brownsville, Tennessee, area along Tennessee State Route 19. He first built a following performing at country dances and fish fries with mandolin player Yank Rachell.

In the 1920s and '30s Hambone Willie showed Sleepy John Estes (from whom most of what is known about Hambone has been gleaned) the ropes on the Mississippi medicine show circuit. While in Atlanta in 1929, Newbern had his sole recording session.

In addition to making the very first known recording of the Delta classic "Roll and Tumble Blues" (later a heavily covered blues standard), Newbern recorded "Shelby County Workhouse Blues" and "Hambone Willie's Dreamy-Eyed Woman's Blues," as well as three rag tunes: "She Could Toodle-Oo," "Nobody Knows (What the Good Deacon Does)," and "Way Down in Arkansas."

Hambone Willie was known to most as an extremely hotheaded man. It surprised few when his bad attitude and behavior put him on a path to prison. A brutal beating in a prison fight when he was in his late forties is the rumored (and likely) cause of Newbern's death.

HAMBONE WILLIE NEWBERN

ROBERT NIGHTHAWK

(ROBERT LEE McCOLLUM, A.K.A. ROBERT LEE McCOY)

MAIN INSTRUMENTS: Slide guitar, vocals, harmonica
BORN: Helena, Arkansas; November 30, 1909
DIED: Helena, Arkansas; November 5, 1967

RECOMMENDED TRACKS: "Black Angel Blues," "Annie Lee," "The Moon Is Rising," "Every Day and Night," "Friars Point Blues"

INTERESTING COVERS: "Black Angel Blues" (as "Sweet Little Angel": Jeff Beck Group; B.B. King)

Robert McCollum left home as a boy to become a street musician. After drifting through southern Mississippi, he stayed awhile in Memphis, Tennessee, where he played with orchestras and groups like the Memphis Jug Band. He performed on Jackson, Mississippi, radio with his cousin and slide guitar mentor Houston Stackhouse.

Robert recorded from the 1930s to the early '40s under several pseudonyms, finally settling on a stage name that came from his first record, "Prowling Night Hawk" (1937). His apparent lack of interest in making records (often going years between sessions) made for huge gaps in his recording career.

After a range of Delta journeys, in the mid-1930s he moved to St. Louis, Missouri, under the name Robert Lee McCoy (his mom's maiden name) to escape some trouble. He played with local bluesmen Henry Townsend, Big Joe Williams, and Sonny Boy Williamson I. They recorded solo and together in 1937 for RCA Victor, which accelerated access to Chicago blues careers for all but McCoy. Robert continued to drift, assuming different names, recording solo and with others, and performing on the radio. Then, he disappeared.

He reemerged years later as electric slide guitar player Robert Nighthawk, recording for Aristocrat, Chess, and other labels. Then he disappeared again.

Nighthawk ultimately seemed to prefer working street corners and tavern one-nighters to playing major gigs like his famous pupils, Muddy Waters and Earl Hooker. He played out on Chicago's Maxwell Street as late as 1964. A 1963 redis-covery of Robert busking in Chicago led to a few more sessions and club dates. After Sonny Boy Williamson II died, Robert briefly took over his *King Biscuit Time* radio show, returning to Helena, Arkansas. He seemed to play every last juke joint he could find until his death at home from congestive heart failure.

TRIVIA: Robert's first Chess session was also Willie Dixon's first Chess session.

ROBERT NIGHTHAWK

JOHNNY OTIS

(JOHN ALEXANDER VELIOTES)

MAIN INSTRUMENTS: Piano, vibraphone, vocals, drums
BORN: Vallejo, California; December 28, 1921
DIED: Los Angeles, California; January 17, 2012

RECOMMENDED TRACKS: "Willie and the Hand Jive," "Double Crossing Blues," "Mistrustin' Blues," "Cupid's Boogie," "Mambo Boogie," "All Nite Long"

INTERESTING COVERS: "Willie and the Hand Jive" (Strangeloves, Eric Clapton)

Teenager John Veliotes, a Greek grocery store owner's son, felt that "Otis" had a blacker sound than "Veliotes," so that's who he became. He moved to Los Angeles during the mid-1940s, where he drummed for the Club Alabam's house band. The club owner pushed Otis to form his own band. Their 1945 record debut, "Harlem Nocturne," was a big-band hit.

Otis backed Wynonie Harris and Charles Brown, then established the Barrelhouse Club in the Watts section of L.A.; Otis became crucial to L.A. His ear for talent found the Robins (a.k.a. the Coasters), Little Esther Phillips, Big Jay McNeely, and Etta James. Otis produced Etta's hit debut, "Roll with Me, Henry," and Big Mama Thornton's original version of "Hound Dog." As a King Records artists and repertoire (A&R) man, he discovered Jackie Wilson, Hank Ballard, and Little Willie John.

Savoy signed Otis in 1949, and he scored ten R&B Top 10 hits (three No. 1s) in that year. At Mercury, his sole hit was a Floyd Dixon cover, "Call Operator 210." His most famous song, "Every Beat of My Heart," a 1952 Royals record, later became a Gladys Knight and the Pips hit. A stint at Peacock from 1953 to 1955 found Otis backing a young Little Richard. A 1958 Bo Diddley–ish Capitol hit, "Willie and the Hand Jive," featuring Johnny on vocals, was his only U.S. Top 10 pop single.

In the late 1950s, Otis hosted his own L.A. TV variety show. He signed with King in 1961, where he also backed Johnny "Guitar" Watson. Otis entered politics in the 1960s and was congressman Mervyn M. Dymally's deputy chief of staff.

Johnny Otis and his blues guitarist son, Shuggie, cut *The New Johnny Otis Show* in 1982. Otis headlined the San Francisco Blues Festival in 1990 and 2000. He founded a gospel church in Santa Rosa and hosted KPFA's *The Johnny Otis Show* well into 2006. He died at home three days before the death of Etta James.

TRIVIA: Frank Zappa cited Otis as the inspiration for his trademark facial hair, according to an interview with *Simpsons* creator Matt Groening.

JOHNNY OTIS

ROBERT PETWAY

MAIN INSTRUMENTS: Guitar, vocals
BORN: Near Yazoo City, Mississippi (or Gee's Bend,
Alabama); 1908, or possibly October 18, 1907
DIED: Chicago, Illinois; possibly May 30, 1978;
(it has not been verified that he has died)

RECOMMENDED TRACKS: "Catfish Blues," "Ride 'Em on Down," "Boogie Woogie Woman"

INTERESTING COVERS: "Catfish Blues" (Muddy Waters as "Rollin' Stone," Jimi Hendrix as both "Catfish Blues" and "Voodoo Chile")

Robert Petway is one of the blues' greatest mysteries. He may have been born at or near a farm by Yazoo City, where his close pal, blues performer Tommy McClennan, was born. Petway followed a typical Delta bluesman path, roaming the land in search of roadhouse and party gigs, both alone and with McClennan.

McClennan settled in Chicago. Petway joined him a few years later to make records. Despite being well respected as a country-blues musician, Petway's recording history is sparse. He cut only eight songs for Chicago's Bluebird Records in 1941, followed by eight more in 1942, of which two were unissued.

One of those songs, however, was "Catfish Blues." Muddy Waters renamed it "Rollin' Stone," an important recording whose title would later provide the name for one of England's greatest rock bands. Jimi Hendrix first recorded the song under its original title, then dramatically reworked it, incorporating chunks of it into his epic blues extravaganza "Voodoo Chile."

Whether or not Petway wrote "Catfish Blues" is in dispute. The song's similarity to McClennan's "Deep Sea Blues" has led historians to believe that Tommy composed it. Bluesman David "Honeyboy" Edwards, a Petway fan who met both Petway and McClennan circa 1930, put forth the claim for Petway. "He just made that song up and used to play it at them old country dances," asserted Edwards. "He just made it up and kept it in his head."

For a long time there was no record of Petway's death. Recent research indicates Robert may have died in Chicago in 1978. If alive, he would be over one hundred years old. According to Honeyboy, "Nobody I know heard what become of him."

TRIVIA: The only known picture of Petway is a 1941 publicity photo.

ROBERT PETWAY

MA RAINEY

(GERTRUDE MALISSA NIX PRIDGETT RAINEY)

MAIN INSTRUMENT: Vocals
BORN: Columbus, Georgia; April 26, 1886 (or September 1882)
DIED: Columbus, Georgia; December 22, 1939

RECOMMENDED TRACKS: "See See Ryder," "Jelly Bean Blues," "Ma Rainey's Black Bottom," "Prove It on Me Blues," "Bo Weavil Blues"

INTERESTING COVERS: "See See Ryder" (Animals as "See See Rider," Mitch Ryder and the Detroit Wheels as incorporated into "Jenny Takes a Ride!")

Gertrude Pridgett first appeared onstage in the Columbus, Georgia, talent show *A Bunch of Blackberries* at age fourteen. She joined a traveling vaudeville troupe, the Rabbit Foot Minstrels, and sang in medicine shows. In 1902, after hearing a sad a cappella song by a rural Missouri girl, Gertrude incorporated this new kind of music into her act, coining a term for it: "the blues."

At age seventeen she married fellow vaudeville singer William "Pa" Rainey and changed her name to "Ma." Ma and Pa danced and sang blues and popular songs at circuses and tent shows all over the South. They became billed as "Rainey and Rainey, Assassinators of the Blues." In 1912 she reputedly took the young Bessie Smith under her wing for three years. By the 1920s Ma Rainey had become popular with both black and white audiences.

Ma's public image was that of a passionate, mistreated lover of men. Her "Prove It on Me Blues" celebrated lesbianism, despite the subject of the song contrasting with her stage persona. Ma was not always careful when it came to hiding her bisexuality, although she usually preferred young men.

After more than twenty years of singing (she was one of the first professional blues singers), the "Mother of the Blues" signed with Paramount in 1923, making her one of the first great female blues singers to record. She cut more than a hundred songs in just six years, many of them true blues classics, backed by jug bands, guitar duos, and bluesmen like Tampa Red and Blind Blake. She also used horns-and-piano jazz bands featuring talents like Louis Armstrong, Kid Ory, and Fletcher Henderson. Rainey's twenty-song collaboration with Thomas Dorsey and two Papa Charlie Jackson duets in 1928 were her last recordings.

Like most classic female blues singers of her era, Ma saw her career decline in the 1930s. Fortunately, she was able to comfortably retire in 1933 and returned to her hometown, where she ran two theaters until her death from a heart attack.

TRIVIA: The U.S. Postal Service issued a Ma Rainey stamp in 1994.

MA RAINEY

JIMMY REED

(MATHIS JAMES REED)

MAIN INSTRUMENTS: Vocals, guitar, harmonica
BORN: Dunleith, Mississippi; September 6, 1925
DIED: Oakland, California; August 29, 1976

RECOMMENDED TRACKS: "Bright Lights, Big City," "Big Boss Man," "Shame Shame Shame," "Ain't That Loving You Baby," "Honest I Do," "I Ain't Got You"

INTERESTING COVERS: "Bright Lights, Big City" (Animals, Rolling Stones), "Big Boss Man" (Pretty Things, Elvis Presley), "Ain't That Loving You Baby" (Beau Brummels), "Honest I Do" (Rolling Stones)

Jimmy Reed was taught the basics of harmonica and guitar by the man who would become his lifelong friend and frequent accompanist, Eddie Taylor. After years of playing Mississippi, Reed arrived in Chicago in 1943 and was drafted into the Navy. He briefly returned to the Delta after WWII and married the love of his life, Mary ("Mama Reed"). Jimmy worked at a Gary, Indiana, meatpacking plant by day until he had established a sizeable following.

Chess Records passed on Jimmy but Vee-Jay picked him up on the recommendation of Albert King, bluesman John Brim's drummer at the time but later a star blues guitarist. At Vee-Jay, Reed hit from the start with "You Don't Have to Go." He landed fourteen Top 20 hits on the R&B charts, eleven of those pop crossovers. Reed's lazy, laid-back singing, piercing, sour harmonica, and deceptively simple guitar shuffles formed one of the most identifiable blues sounds of the 1950s and '60s. His easy-to-play-but-difficult-to-master hits became some of the most covered blues songs of all time.

Despite Mama Reed's loyal support, Reed's illiteracy, the brutal road life of a bluesman, and severe alcoholism (he described himself as a "liquor glutter") all worked against him. At performances, Mary Reed often discreetly whispered lyrics to Jimmy, who had forgotten them in his alcoholic haze onstage; she can even be heard on some of his recordings. His behavior became painfully embarrassing; some of it was a result of undiagnosed epilepsy, disguised by his frequent spells of the d.t.'s (delirium tremens).

After Vee-Jay went under, Jimmy's streak of hits ended. Following one last European tour in 1968 with the American Folk Blues Festival, he withdrew from the public. His epilepsy finally got properly treated and he quit drinking, but by then it was too late. He tried to make a comeback via blues festivals but died in the process.

JIMMY REED

BLIND JOE REYNOLDS

(JOE SHEPPARD, JOE LEONARD)

MAIN INSTRUMENTS: Vocals, guitar
BORN: Tallulah, Louisiana (possibly Arkansas); 1904 (or 1900)
DIED: Monroe, Louisiana; March 10, 1968

RECOMMENDED TRACK: "Outside Woman Blues"

INTERESTING COVER: "Outside Woman Blues" (Cream)

Louisiana street singer Joe Sheppard, whose nephew said his real name was Joe Leonard, created recording aliases to keep one step ahead of the law and for "escaping enemies." Blinded in the mid-1920s by a shotgun blast to the face, Joe, amazingly, was also known for his accuracy with a pistol. He claimed he could discern the location of a target by sound alone.

It was no secret in the South that Reynolds held an open hostility toward the legal system and the police (he had served two jail terms), had complete disdain for traditional morality, and never lost his relish for trouble. His music is known for the eerie, high-pitched wail of his vocals, the driving, hypnotic roll of his rhythmic slide playing, and his lyrics, usually about unfaithful women.

Reynolds performed for years on street corners before being discovered in 1929 by a Memphis record shop owner and talent scout, who contacted Paramount Records. As Blind Joe Reynolds, he cut two records in a small Wisconsin studio: "Outside Woman Blues"/"Nehi Blues" and "Cold Woman Blues"/"99 Blues," the latter the holy grail of blues collectors because of its rarity. Paramount never called him back to record again, but he made a couple more records when the RCA Victor truck arrived in Memphis the following year. As Blind Willie Reynolds, he recorded "Third Street Woman Blues" and "Married Man Blues." His other two songs, "Short Dress Blues" and "Goose Hill Woman Blues," weren't issued and are perhaps lost forever. These eight songs were Reynolds's sole recorded output.

In 1967 the U.K. band Cream recorded "Outside Woman Blues" on their LP *Disraeli Gears*. Blind Joe died from pneumonia less than a year later, just missing his seat on the folk-blues festival carousel.

TRIVIA: "Cold Woman Blues" was thought lost forever until 2000, when a copy surfaced that was bought in 1976 by an Ohio music teacher at a Nashville flea market for one dollar. He resold his copy for $5,500. It is still the only one known to exist. Cream oddly credited "Arthur Reynolds" with "Outside Woman Blues."

BLIND JOE REYNOLDS

JIMMY ROGERS

(JAMES A. LANE)

MAIN INSTRUMENTS: Vocals, guitar, harmonica
BORN: Ruleville, Mississippi; June 3, 1924
DIED: Chicago, Illinois; December 19, 1997

RECOMMENDED TRACKS: "That's All Right," "Walking by Myself," "Money, Marbles and Chalk," "Left Me with a Broken Heart," "Act Like You Love Me," "Chicago Bound"

INTERESTING COVER: "Walking by Myself" (Gary Moore)

Jimmy Lane was raised in Mississippi, Atlanta, West Memphis, Memphis, and St. Louis, learning harp and guitar as a teen with childhood chum Snooky Pryor. Jimmy took his stepfather's last name, then played in early-1940s Chicago with Big Bill Broonzy, Sonny Boy Williamson, and Sunnyland Slim. His first record (1946) was miscredited to "Memphis Slim and His House-rockers."

Rogers's premier record as a band leader was for Ora-Nelle in 1947; his subsequent Apollo and Regal work went unreleased. Leonard Chess noticed those bad business calls, and with Rogers backed by Little Walter, the 1950 classic "That's All Right" was the first of several Rogers hits for Chess.

The addition of Muddy Waters changed Jimmy's and guitarist Blue Smitty's duo into a trio. When Smitty split, Rogers gave the harp spot to Little Walter and switched to second guitar. This explosive postwar Chicago blues band was referred to as the Headcutters or the Headhunters because their superior chops stole the stage—and jobs—from other local bands. Jimmy first recorded with Muddy in 1949 and backed him for another six years, when Rogers left to lead his own band. His only R&B chart hit was a version of T-Bone Walker's "Why Not," rewritten by Jimmy as 1957's "Walking by Myself."

In the early 1960s a brief time with Howlin' Wolf preceded Jimmy's leaving showbiz. He drove a cab and owned a clothing store that got torched in the riots sparked by the assassination of Dr. Martin Luther King Jr. Rogers resumed touring in 1971 and was soon back in the studio for Leon Russell's Shelter label. He recorded his first LP there, *Gold-Tailed Bird*, backed by Freddie King. Jimmy reunited with Muddy for a 1977 session, and continued to record and tour right up until he died from colon cancer.

TRIVIA: Rogers lived the longest of all of Muddy Waters's first, great Chicago band. At the time of his death, he was recording *Blues, Blues, Blues* with Eric Clapton, Keith Richards, Taj Mahal, Robert Plant, Jimmy Page, and Mick Jagger.

JIMMY ROGERS

BESSIE SMITH

MAIN INSTRUMENT: Vocals
BORN: Chattanooga, Tennessee; April 15, 1894
DIED: Clarksdale, Mississippi; September 26, 1937

RECOMMENDED TRACKS: "Downhearted Blues," "St. Louis Blues," "Empty Bed Blues," "Gimme a Pigfoot," "Nobody Knows You When You're Down and Out," "I Ain't Got Nobody," "Gin House Blues," "I Need a Little Sugar in My Bowl"

INTERESTING COVERS: "St. Louis Blues" (Cab Calloway), "Gin House Blues" (Animals, Nina Simone), "Tain't Nobody's Business If I Do" (Billie Holiday), "Nobody Knows You When You're Down and Out" (Spencer Davis Group, Otis Redding), "I Ain't Got Nobody" (Louis Prima, David Lee Roth)

Bessie Smith's parents died before she was ten. She and her brother Andrew began performing on the streets, primarily in front of Chattanooga's White Elephant Saloon. In 1904 her brother Clarence left home for the Moses Stokes troupe. In 1912, Bessie became a dancer in the group because Ma Rainey was already Stokes's singer. Ma trained Bessie in stagecraft and she quickly improved upon what Rainey had taught her. Smith wed a security guard, then left her rocky marriage, never divorcing, to live with Richard Morgan (Lionel Hampton's uncle) until her death.

In 1923 Bessie signed with Columbia. Her first record, Alberta Hunter's "Downhearted Blues," was a huge hit. She made about 160 recordings for Columbia. The top headliner on the Theater Owners Booking Association circuit, Bessie was the highest-paid black entertainer of her time.

Smith's only film was the 1929 short *St. Louis Blues*. "Talkies" ended vaudeville. Though she was at the peak of her powers and had never stopped touring, Columbia dropped her. John Hammond recorded her last session after seeing her in a club. Smith's potential comeback, appearing in Hammond's first *From Spirituals to Swing* concert in 1938, was foiled by a Mississippi car accident; she never regained consciousness. Seven thousand people attended her funeral.

The greatest, most popular and influential female blues singer of the 1920s and '30s, "the Empress of the Blues" was the first major blues and jazz singer on record (the first blues vocal recorded by an African American singer was 1920's "Crazy Blues" by Mamie Smith), preceding Ma Rainey by half a year.

TRIVIA: Bessie's embittered first husband pocketed the money raised to purchase her gravestone. Her grave was left unmarked until rock singer Janis Joplin and Juanita Green (who as a child did housework for Smith) paid for a tombstone in 1970.

BESSIE SMITH

CLARA SMITH

MAIN INSTRUMENT: Vocals
BORN: Spartanburg County, South Carolina; ca. 1894
DIED: Detroit, Michigan; February 2, 1935

RECOMMENDED TRACKS: "Whip It to a Jelly," "It's Tight Like That," "Wanna Go Home," "Ol' Sam Tages," "Living Humble," "Gin Mill Blues"

Clara Smith started her singing career on the African American theater circuit and in tent shows. She jumped into vaudeville around 1910, honing her theater craft as she traveled throughout the South. By the end of the decade she was a Theater Owners Booking Association circuit headliner.

In 1923 Clara was working the New York cabarets and speakeasies. She recorded for Columbia from 1923 to 1932—one of the few classic blues singers able to continue recording during the Depression. Smith cut 122 songs, often backed by talent such as Louis Armstrong and Fletcher Henderson. She dueted twice on record with label mate Bessie Smith and four times with Lonnie Johnson. Clara had a volatile friendship with Bessie; at one party they had an argument that ended with Bessie knocking Clara out with a punch to the nose.

Although Clara was promoted as "the World's Champion Moaner," her voice was actually more delicate, sensual, and affectionate than those of most of her competitors. She toured all over the United States and starred in Harlem revues during her best years. She opened her own Harlem jazz and blues spot, the Clara Smith Theatrical Club. In 1933 Clara moved to Detroit, Michigan, where she sang at local theaters until she was hospitalized for heart disease. Smith passed away from heart failure.

It's not surprising that Clara is compared to the other Smiths from her era, Bessie and Mamie (all unrelated). Despite her superb roster of backing musicians, Clara's musical support was not as consistent as Bessie Smith's, nor did she have a voice as imposing as Bessie's. But then, who did?

TRIVIA: Young Josephine Baker was Clara's assistant and was rumored to be her lover.

CLARA SMITH

CLARENCE "PINE TOP" (OR "PINETOP") SMITH

MAIN INSTRUMENTS: Piano, vocals
BORN: Troy, Alabama; June 11, 1904
DIED: Chicago, Illinois; March 15, 1929

RECOMMENDED TRACK: "Pine Top's Boogie Woogie"

INTERESTING COVERS: "Pine Top's Boogie Woogie" (Gene Taylor, Bob Thiele Orchestra, Tommy Dorsey and His Orchestra as "Boogie Woogie")

Clarence Smith was nicknamed "Pine Top" because he was such an avid tree climber as a boy. Musically self-taught, he performed at Birmingham house parties as a teen until he moved to Pittsburgh, Pennsylvania, in 1920. After working there, he performed music and comedy on the Theater Owners Booking Association vaudeville circuit tours, then was the piano accompanist for Ma Rainey and for Butterbeans and Susie. Cow Cow Davenport tipped off Vocalion Records, and in 1928 Pine Top moved to Chicago to take them up on their recording offer. His Chicago apartment neighbors, Albert Ammons and Pete Johnson, cited Smith as a key influence and they frequently jammed together.

In 1928 Smith recorded his vigorous hit "Pine Top's Boogie Woogie," the first recorded use of the term "boogie-woogie." Pine Top was the first to implore "the girl with the red dress on" to "shake that thing."

The day before his second Vocalion session, Smith's bright career ended when he was killed by a stray shot fired during a dancehall ruckus ("I SAW PINETOP SPIT BLOOD" was the famous *Down Beat* headline). Although he recorded only eleven tracks, Smith ranks among the most influential blues icons of the 1920s.

TRIVIA: Pine Top's legacy was enhanced when Tommy Dorsey and His Orchestra's 1938 big band arrangement of "Boogie Woogie" became Dorsey's biggest hit (over five million copies sold). In 1975 the Bob Thiele Orchestra recorded *I Saw Pinetop Spit Blood*, a modern jazz LP that included the lurid title song and a cover of "Pine Top's Boogie Woogie."

No photos of Smith exist, so I depicted a man twenty-five years old with a medium-to-slender build because of his age and because no reference is made to his being overweight (his name was not prefaced with the popular adjectives for large people, "Big" or the ironic "Tiny"). Most musicians seemed to have smoked back then, hence the cigarette, the smoke of which obscures his unknown facial features.

VICTORIA SPIVEY

MAIN INSTRUMENTS: Vocals, piano, organ, ukulele
BORN: Houston, Texas; October 15, 1906
DIED: New York, New York; October 3, 1976

RECOMMENDED TRACKS: "Dope Head Blues," "TB Blues," "Black Snake Blues"

Victoria Regina Spivey's first professional experience was in her father's family string band. Her sisters, "Sweet Pea" and Elton Island, both had professional singing careers. In 1918, Victoria left home to accompany films on piano at the Lincoln Theatre in Dallas, Texas. In her teens, she played Galveston and Houston gambling dens, gay clubs, and whorehouses, solo and with Blind Lemon Jefferson.

In 1926 Victoria relocated to St. Louis, Missouri. Her first record, "Black Snake Blues" on OKeh, had healthy sales. Ida Cox's music inspired Spivey's drug-related and sexually provocative lyrics. Victoria also counted Sara Martin, Bessie Smith, and Bobby "Blue" Bland among her influences.

Spivey recorded in New York for OKeh until 1929, when she signed with RCA Victor, Vocalion, and Decca. Director King Vidor cast her in his first sound film, 1929's *Hallelujah!* Throughout the 1930s and '40s, Spivey toured with Louis Armstrong and worked in musical films and stage shows, including the *Hellzapoppin' Revue*, often alongside her dancer husband, Billy Adams.

In 1951 Spivey retired from the commercial music business to play and sing in her church. Her secular return was singing for her old partner Lonnie Johnson on his 1961 *Idle Hours* LP. She recorded *Songs We Taught Your Mother* with fellow blues vets Alberta Hunter and Lucille Hegamin. She returned to nightclub work and took advantage of the 1960s blues revival, singing at folk and blues festivals. In 1962 she founded her blues-related label, Spivey Records. Two of her company's releases featured Spivey and Big Joe Williams supported by Bob Dylan on harmonica and backup vocals. Victoria's risqué and drug-referencing lyrics made her immediately popular with blues audiences in the 1960s and well into the '70s.

Spivey died from an internal hemorrhage.

TRIVIA: Victoria Spivey mentored Maria Muldaur and wrote a glowing review of Muldaur's first appearance at the Newport Folk Festival for *Record Research*.

VICTORIA SPIVEY

SUNNYLAND SLIM

(ALBERT LUANDREW)

MAIN INSTRUMENTS: Piano, vocals
BORN: Quitman County (near Vance), Mississippi;
September 5, 1906 (not 1907, as is often reported)
DIED: Chicago, Illinois; March 17, 1995

RECOMMENDED TRACKS: "Illinois Central," "Sweet Lucy Blues," "Shake It Baby,"
"Brownskin Woman," "It's You Baby," "Sunnyland Train"

Born on a farm, Albert Luandrew first learned keyboards on a pump organ. He played Delta juke joints and movie houses, then moved to Memphis in 1925. Performing on Beale Street, he befriended Little Brother Montgomery and Ma Rainey.

Luandrew's stage name came from his physical build and one of his best-known songs, "Sunnyland Train," about a deadly St. Louis-to-Memphis locomotive that often mowed down folks who attempted to cross its tracks.

Sunnyland Slim was one of many Southern workers who migrated north for work in Chicago in 1939. His freelance keyboard skills put him in demand. Slim's premier recording, as a Jump Jackson band singer in 1946, was followed in 1947 by his first recordings as a leader. He played with Sonny Boy Williamson I before cutting eight solo songs for RCA Victor as "Doctor Clayton's Buddy." Over the years, Sunnyland played with Howlin' Wolf, Robert Lockwood Jr., and Little Walter.

Between 1948 and 1956 Slim sessioned and solo-recorded with more than a dozen labels. In 1960 he cut his debut LP, *Slim's Shout*, with King Curtis backing him on sax. Slim founded his own label, Airway Records. He recorded *Chicago Jump* for Red Beans in 1985, backed by the same band that had played with him every Sunday evening for twelve years at the North Side Chicago club B.L.U.E.S.

Despite many bouts of illness, Slim continued to perform. In 1995, he slipped on some ice on his way home from a gig, complications of which eventually led to his dying of kidney failure.

TRIVIA: At Sunnyland Slim's Aristocrat session in 1947, he introduced the Chess brothers to Muddy Waters.

SUNNYLAND SLIM

TAMPA RED

(HUDSON WOODBRIDGE, A.K.A. HUDSON WHITTAKER)

MAIN INSTRUMENTS: Guitar, vocals
BORN: Smithville, Georgia; January 8, 1904
DIED: Chicago, Illinois; March 19, 1981

RECOMMENDED TRACKS: "It Hurts Me Too," "Love Her with a Feeling," "It's Tight Like That," "Let Me Play with Your Poodle," "Don't You Lie to Me"

INTERESTING COVERS: "It's Tight Like That" (Clara Smith), "It Hurts Me Too" (Elmore James), "Don't You Lie to Me" (Chuck Berry, Albert King, Gary Moore)

Street musician Piccolo Pete taught orphan Hudson Woodbridge his first blues licks, and by the 1920s Hudson had perfected his unique single-string slide technique (a blues and rock guitar solo precursor). He began his professional career in Chicago as Tampa Red, a name derived from his childhood home and light skin. He became Ma Rainey's accompanist, recording humorous, sexually salty songs (called "hokum") like their 1928 classic "It's Tight Like That."

Most of Tampa Red's early recordings were made with Georgia Tom Dorsey. They released nearly ninety recordings, some as the Hokum Boys and others (with Frankie "Half Pint" Jaxon) as Tampa Red's Hokum Jug Band. After their partnership ended in 1932, Red carried on as a session musician, working with Sonny Boy Williamson I and Memphis Minnie.

In 1934 Red signed with RCA Victor, where he remained for nineteen years. After going electric, his single "Let Me Play with Your Poodle" (1942) hit No. 4 on Billboard's Harlem Hit Parade.

Red played every down-home and upscale venue imaginable. According to close pals Big Maceo Merriweather and Big Bill Broonzy, Red turned his home into a blues community center. As the popularity of that genre grew and farm employment in the South dwindled, Red casually provided rehearsal space, bookings, meals, and lodging for musicians who flowed into Chicago from the Delta.

His career was given new life in the late 1950s by the blues revival. Red took up booze after his wife's death in 1953 and died in poverty.

TRIVIA: Tampa Red became billed as "the Man with the Gold Guitar" and "the Guitar Wizard" because in 1928 he became the first black musician to play a National steel-body resonator guitar, acquiring a gold-plated model in their first year available. Nationals were the loudest and fanciest guitars prior to amplification. Red's original National is on display at the Experience Music Project.

TAMPA RED

ARTHUR "MONTANA" TAYLOR

MAIN INSTRUMENTS: Piano, vocals
BORN: Butte, Montana; 1903
DIED: Whereabouts unknown; 1954

RECOMMENDED TRACKS: "Indiana Avenue Stomp," "Detroit Rocks," "I Can't Sleep"

INTERESTING TRIBUTE: Classical piano composer David Matthews created a short tribute piece titled "Montana Taylor's Blues."

A big fish in a small blues pond, Arthur Taylor is considered the finest blues pianist and the best blues artist ever to emerge from Montana. He was famed as one of the most authoritative lowdown-and-dirty barrelhouse boogie players.

Arthur was exposed to live music at an early age: his dad owned a club in Butte. In 1919 the Taylors moved to Chicago and Indianapolis, Indiana, where Arthur was taught piano at age sixteen. He played whatever coffee shop, nightclub, and rent party gigs came his way before moving to Cleveland, Ohio, and then back to Chicago. In 1929, he recorded two singles for Vocalion.

His copyrights and first recording rights slipped through his talented fingers and ended up in the hands of a flurry of small record labels. Taylor may hold the dubious distinction of being stolen from more than any other blues artist. Discouraged by his lack of royalties, Arthur disappeared. Some say he gave up piano.

After rediscovery by a fan in 1946, Taylor, still in top form, cut new solo material and supported Bertha "Chippie" Hill. He had improved as a singer, too, especially on blues ballads. Taylor, however, once again became overwhelmed by discouragement with the music business. After a final recorded appearance on a 1948 radio broadcast, Taylor vanished once more, this time for good.

TRIVIA: The Rolling Stones' guitarist Bill Wyman credits Taylor's "Indiana Avenue Stomp" as a key inspiration in his becoming a musician.

MONTANA TAYLOR

SONNY TERRY
& BROWNIE McGHEE
(SAUNDERS TERRELL & WALTER BROWN McGHEE)

MAIN INSTRUMENTS: Guitar (Sonny), harmonica (Brownie)
BORN: Greensboro, North Carolina; October 24, 1911 (Sonny);
Knoxville, Tennessee; November 30, 1915 (Brownie)
DIED: Mineola, New York; March 11, 1986 (Sonny);
Oakland, California; February 16, 1996 (Brownie)

RECOMMENDED TRACKS: "I'm Gonna Rock," "John Henry," "Hootin' the Blues"

B y sixteen, Sonny Terry was blind from two injuries. Forced to rely on his harmonica skills, he played for tips in Raleigh and Durham, North Carolina, and befriended Blind Boy Fuller in 1934. The duo became popular instantly. They recorded for Vocalion in 1937, then Terry was invited to perform in John Hammond's first *From Spirituals to Swing* Carnegie Hall concert in 1938. Back in Durham, through Fuller, Terry met Brownie McGhee.

McGhee was raised in Kingsport, Tennessee, and contracted polio at age four. His uncle created his first guitar from a tin marshmallow box and a board. In 1937, an operation funded by the March of Dimes restored McGhee's ability to walk. McGhee was initially sent for by Fuller's manager to be Sonny's assistant. Sonny and Brownie each first recorded in 1940.

Following Fuller's death, McGhee cut "Death of Blind Boy Fuller." Columbia renamed him "Blind Boy Fuller No. 2" to continue Blind Boy's sales. McGhee's third OKeh session was his first with Sonny Terry. They instantly found work in New York as a duo and solo. Terry played on Lead Belly, Woody Guthrie, and Pete Seeger gigs. McGhee landed a 1948 No. 2 R&B hit with "My Fault." Two of the first bluesmen to regularly play 1950s Europe, Sonny and Brownie toured, together and then separately, eleven months out of the year from 1958 to 1980, recording dozens of LPs.

Their partnership ended in the mid-1970s, after which they wouldn't even share a stage. McGhee died from stomach cancer while semiretired. Terry wrote the book *The Harp Styles of Sonny Terry* and traveled. After 1980 he quit recording. He died just before he was inducted into the Blues Foundation's Hall of Fame.

TRIVIA: McGhee appeared in *Angel Heart*. Terry was in *The Color Purple*. Both were in the original Broadway cast of *Cat on a Hot Tin Roof*. McGhee's brother Stick hit with "Drinkin' Wine Spo-Dee-O-Dee."

SONNY **TERRY** & BROWNIE **McGHEE**

HENRY THOMAS

(A.K.A. RAGTIME TEXAS)

MAIN INSTRUMENTS: Vocals, guitar, quills
BORN: Big Sandy, Texas; 1874
DIED: Whereabouts unknown (possibly Texas); 1950s (?)

RECOMMENDED TRACKS: "Bull Doze Blues," "Fishin' Blues"

INTERESTING COVERS: "Bull Doze Blues" (Canned Heat as "Going Up the Country"),
"Fishin' Blues" (Taj Mahal, Lovin' Spoonful, Chris Thomas King), "Don't Ease Me
In" (Grateful Dead), "Honey Won't You Allow Me One More Chance" (Bob Dylan as
"Honey Just Allow Me One More Chance")

History indicates Henry Thomas left home in his teens and became a
wandering street musician, riding the rails across Texas and perhaps visiting
the World Fairs that took place in St. Louis and Chicago around 1900. Like
those of his younger peers Charley Patton and Lead Belly, Henry's collection
of songs melded African American musical styles from the two centuries. He
recorded spirituals, ballads, reels, dance songs, and eight blues tracks, all meant
to appeal to both black and white audiences.

Thomas capoed his guitar high on its neck and played it like a banjo, preferring rhythmic strumming to fingerpicking. At the same time, he played the quills,
a common but rarely recorded panpipe-type African American folk instrument
indigenous to Mississippi, Louisiana, and Texas, constructed from cane reeds.
They can be heard on Thomas's famous "Bull Doze Blues" intro (re-created forty
years later in "Going Up the Country," Canned Heat's version of the song).

Henry is generally considered to be the earliest African American folk artist
to produce a meaningful recorded legacy. But after cutting twenty-three timeless
songs for Vocalion in 1927 through 1929, he slid back into obscurity. His whereabouts after 1929 are unknown, though there is one report of his being seen in
Texas in the 1950s.

TRIVIA: "Last Night I Dreamed of Henry Thomas" was a song on Deacon Blue's
1993 album *Whatever You Say, Say Nothing*.

HENRY THOMAS

BIG MAMA THORNTON

(WILLIE MAE THORNTON)

MAIN INSTRUMENTS: Vocals, harmonica, drums
BORN: Montgomery, Alabama; December 11, 1926
DIED: Los Angeles, California; July 25, 1984

RECOMMENDED TRACKS: "Hound Dog," "Ball 'n' Chain," "Chauffeur Blues," "Mercy," "My Heavy Load"

INTERESTING COVERS: "Hound Dog" (Elvis Presley), "Ball 'n' Chain" (Big Brother and the Holding Company), "Chauffeur Blues" (Jefferson Airplane)

After her hymn-singing mother died, Willie Mae left Montgomery at fourteen to tour for seven years with the Georgia-based Hot Harlem Revue. In 1948, she settled in Houston, Texas, to advance her career.

Thornton first recorded in 1951 for Peacock Records with producer Johnny Otis. They also recorded "Hound Dog," reputedly a gift to her from composers Jerry Leiber and Mike Stoller. It remained at No. 1 on the R&B charts for seven weeks. Elvis Presley's 1956 cover was even bigger, somewhat derailing Big Mama's bid for musical immortality. Thornton cut a series of fine singles through 1957, during her time touring with Junior Parker and Esther Phillips, but she never had another hit. Her career soon began to fade and she moved to the San Francisco area. She sought harmonica session work and played local blues clubs in the first half of the 1960s, recording occasionally for small labels.

In 1966 she recorded *Big Mama Thornton with the Muddy Waters Blues Band*. Her 1968 LP, *Ball 'n' Chain*, recorded with Lightnin' Hopkins and Larry Williams (and later boosted by Janis Joplin's cover of "Ball 'n' Chain"), as well as two 1969–70 Mercury albums, had her back working concerts and blues festivals across America and Europe from 1966 until her death; she continued to record for a number of labels in the 1970s.

After years of heavy drinking, Big Mama died of a heart attack; her body was discovered by medics in an L.A. rooming house.

Big Mama liked to cross-dress and had no patience for foolish opinions on this and many other matters. She carried on the tough "blues mama" tradition of Bessie Smith, Memphis Minnie, and Ma Rainey.

TRIVIA: Thornton often simultaneously played drums and harmonica onstage. She was one of two witnesses who saw blues singer Johnny Ace accidentally shoot himself to death.

BIG MAMA THORNTON

BESSIE TUCKER

MAIN INSTRUMENT: Vocals
BORN: East Texas (perhaps Greenville?); date unknown
DIED: Whereabouts unknown; date unknown

RECOMMENDED TRACKS: "Penitentiary," "Fryin' Pan Skillet Blues"

A light-complexioned, delicate woman with a big, earthy voice and a tough-as-nails reputation, Bessie Tucker was influenced by the folk and field holler vocal traditions of her East Texas region. Researchers have deduced from her song lyrics that she was perhaps based in Greenville, Texas, but most of her life (and her death) remains a mystery.

The recordings of Bessie, Victoria Spivey, Texas Alexander, and Texas Bill Day all reflected the same Texas style. Given her slight frame and powerful voice, she has been described as a "female equivalent to Charlie Patton."

A bawdy 1928 Memphis session (possibly shared with Ida May Mack) for the RCA Victor label is responsible for Tucker's place in blues history, resulting in her best-known and apparently somewhat autobiographical song, "Penitentiary," backed by Dallas pianist K. D. Johnson.

A final recording date, this time with Johnson and guitarist Jesse Thomas, took place the next year, after which Tucker seems to have stopped performing. Nothing else is known about Bessie since completing her recorded legacy of twenty-four blues and country tracks, which includes seven alternate takes.

TRIVIA: Only one photograph of Bessie Tucker survives.

BESSIE TUCKER

BIG JOE TURNER

(JOSEPH VERNON TURNER JR.)

MAIN INSTRUMENT: Vocals
BORN: Kansas City, Missouri; May 18, 1911
DIED: Inglewood, California; November 24, 1985

RECOMMENDED TRACKS: "Roll 'Em, Pete," "Honey Hush," "Shake, Rattle and Roll," "Flip Flop and Fly," "Cherry Red," "Wee Baby Blues," "Midnight Special"

INTERESTING COVERS: "Honey Hush" (Johnny Burnette Trio, Fleetwood Mac), "Shake, Rattle and Roll" (Bill Haley and His Comets, Elvis Presley), "Corrine, Corrina" (Taj Mahal), "Lipstick, Powder and Paint" (Shakin' Stevens)

Big Joe Turner weighed three hundred–plus pounds and stood six feet two inches tall. This premier postwar blues shouter led the transition from big bands to jump blues to R&B and to rock 'n' roll, all with great success. "The Boss of the Blues" came by his love of music through the church. Joe sang in the streets for tips, then left school at fourteen to work in Kansas City clubs. As "the Singing Barman," Turner and boogie master Pete Johnson became resident partners at local clubs. Joe's shouts could shake, rattle, and roll any gin joint—without the aid of a microphone.

In 1938 John Hammond invited them to appear in his *From Spirituals to Swing* Carnegie Hall concert. They launched a boogie-woogie craze that resulted in a Café Society residency. Their hit, "Roll 'Em Pete," has one of the first recorded examples of accented syncopation known as a "backbeat."

Turner performed in Duke Ellington's revue *Jump for Joy* and in short musical films. In 1945 the doors opened on Joe and Pete's own L.A. bar, the Blue Moon Club. A National Records cover of "S.K. Blues" was Joe's first national R&B hit. He also recorded for Imperial, backed by Fats Domino. With the exception of "My Gal's a Jockey" and "Still in the Dark," Turner's late 1940s to early '50s records sold poorly.

In 1951 Atlantic's Ertegun brothers spotted Big Joe playing with Count Basie at the Apollo Theater and signed him. "Chains of Love" was a smash, and he suddenly became a hit machine. "Honey Hush" was his first R&B No. 1, in 1953; his second, "Shake, Rattle and Roll," turned him into a teen rock star a year later. He appeared in the 1956 film *Shake, Rattle and Rock!* After 1958, his popularity waned.

In the 1960s and '70s Turner was celebrated at blues festivals. He cut 1983's *Blues Train* with Roomful of Blues. Despite size-related health issues, he toured until shortly before his death from a heart attack.

BIG JOE TURNER

T-BONE WALKER

(AARON THIBEAUX WALKER)

MAIN INSTRUMENTS: Guitar, vocals
BORN: Linden, Texas; May 26, 1910
DIED: Los Angeles, California; March 16, 1975

RECOMMENDED TRACKS: "Call It Stormy Monday (But Tuesday Is Just as Bad),"
"T-Bone Shuffle," "T-Bone Jumps Again," "West Side Baby," "The Hustle Is On,"
"Cold Cold Feeling," "Railroad Station Blues," "Two Bones and a Pick"

INTERESTING COVERS: "Call It Stormy Monday (But Tuesday Is Just as Bad)" (Them
as "Stormy Monday Blues," Chris Farlowe and the Thunderbirds), "Two Bones and
a Pick" (Blues Band)

Both of Aaron Walker's African American and Cherokee parents were musicians. The teen guitarist befriended and led family friend Blind Lemon Jefferson from bar to bar as Lemon played for tips. Walker debuted on Columbia as Oak Cliff T-Bone in 1929, then headed west for Los Angeles.

By 1939 Walker was playing L.A.'s Central Avenue hotspots. He sang (but didn't play the guitar) on "T-Bone Blues" with Les Hite for Varsity Records in 1940. T-Bone formed his own band and recorded his first Capitol single, "Mean Old World," raising the musical bar with his sophisticated guitar work and mature, laid-back vocals. In 1946 he began racking up the blues classics, including 1947's "Call It Stormy Monday (But Tuesday Is Just as Bad)" from his 1946 to '48 period on Black & White Records. His hits on Imperial (1950 to '54) were produced by Dave Bartholomew. Atlantic's *T-Bone Blues* LP was recorded in sessions in 1955 (with Junior Wells and Jimmy Rogers), 1956, and 1957.

T-Bone's popularity sank with the rise of rock. He headlined the first American Folk Blues Festival in Europe in 1962. Acclaimed 1968 and 1969 LPs brought him new notice. He continued recording from 1968 through 1975, scoring a 1971 Grammy Award for Polydor's *Good Feelin'*. Stomach issues and a stroke in 1974 crippled his career. After a second stroke, he died from bronchial pneumonia.

TRIVIA: T-Bone Walker was the first bluesman to record with an electric guitar. B.B. King is quoted as saying that hearing "Stormy Monday Blues" prompted him to buy his first electric guitar. Chuck Berry cited Walker and Louis Jordan as his two key influences. T-Bone's stage tricks of playing guitar with his teeth and behind his back inspired Jimi Hendrix. After playing a Walker session, Jimmy Rogers adapted T-Bone's "Why Not" as his own hit "Walking by Myself." Walker's nephew was jazzman Barney Kessel.

T-BONE WALKER

SIPPIE WALLACE

(BEULAH THOMAS)

MAIN INSTRUMENT: Vocals
BORN: Houston, Texas; November 1, 1898
DIED: Detroit, Michigan; November 1, 1986

RECOMMENDED TRACKS: "I'm a Mighty Tight Woman," "Women Be Wise," "Special Delivery Blues," "Bedroom Blues," "Up the Country Blues"

INTERESTING COVER: "Women Be Wise" (Bonnie Raitt)

One of thirteen kids of a Baptist deacon, Sippie Thomas was born into a musical family. She sang and played piano in church and as a young girl began performing at tent shows as "the Texas Nightingale" with her younger brother, Hersal Thomas, on piano. By her mid-teens, she had left Houston with Hersal for New Orleans to build a following. Sippie married Matt Wallace and followed brothers Hersal and George to Chicago in 1923, where she was snapped up by OKeh Records. Her first two recordings, "Shorty George" and "Up the Country Blues," made Sippie a star.

The 1920s saw hits backed by Louis Armstrong, Sidney Bechet, and King Oliver. Her OKeh contract expired in 1929, and she moved to Detroit, then ceased recording and most performing. Her brothers and her husband had died by 1936. As its organist, singer, and choir director, Detroit's Leland Baptist Church was just about Sippie's sole performance platform for the next three decades.

In 1966 Wallace sang on *Louis Armstrong and the Blues Singers* and was lured by her friend Victoria Spivey to join the flourishing blues festival circuit and return to the studio. Sippie's first new LP was of duets with Spivey. Roosevelt Sykes and Little Brother Montgomery played on her LPs *Women Be Wise* and *Sippie Wallace Sings the Blues*.

In 1970 Sippie suffered a stroke, which slowed but did not stop her recording and performing. In 1982 Bonnie Raitt produced *Sippie*, scoring a Grammy nomination and winning the W.C. Handy Award for the year's best blues album. After a 1983 LP with German boogie-woogie pianist Axel Zwingenberger, they recorded her only complete live album, *An Evening with Sippie Wallace*. Sippie suffered a bad stroke in Germany after a 1986 jazz festival concert. She was hospitalized and returned to the United States, dying on her eighty-eighth birthday.

TRIVIA: Sippie appeared in the 1982 documentary *Jammin' with the Blues Greats* and was the subject of the 1983 doc, *Sippie Wallace: Blues Singer and Song Writer*.

SIPPIE WALLACE

WASHBOARD SAM

(ROBERT BROWN)

MAIN INSTRUMENTS: Washboard, vocals
BORN: Walnut Ridge, Arkansas; July 15, 1910
DIED: Chicago, Illinois; November 6, 1966

RECOMMENDED TRACKS: "Mama Don't Allow It," "Back Door," "Diggin' My Potatoes," "My Bucket's Got a Hole in It"

INTERESTING COVERS: "Mama Don't Allow It" (J. J. Cale, Arthur Crudup), "My Bucket's Got a Hole in It" (Hank Williams, Louis Armstrong, Ricky Nelson)

Washboard Sam, the illegitimate half-brother of Big Bill Broonzy, grew up in Arkansas, working on a farm. In the early 1920s he played the streets of Memphis with Sleepy John Estes and Hammie Nixon. In 1932 he moved to Chicago and partnered regularly with Big Bill Broonzy at gigs, and eventually on Broonzy's recordings. Sam became a hot Bluebird Records session man, and played with Tampa Red and Memphis Slim.

In 1935 Washboard began his solo recording career, often supported by Broonzy. Between 1935 and 1949 Sam recorded more than 160 songs, becoming one of America's most popular Chicago bluesmen of that era. He boasted huge record sales and sold-out shows, thanks to his powerful voice and songwriting talent.

After WWII, Sam had difficulty dealing with the electric changeover. His audience shrank. His final RCA Victor session was in 1949, and he recorded one last 1953 Chess session with Broonzy and Memphis Slim. He retired from music that year and studied to become a Chicago police officer.

Sam initially resisted the efforts of Willie Dixon and Memphis Slim to convince him to take advantage of the early-1960s blues revival, but he began playing in Chicago clubs and coffeehouses in 1963, and at European venues in 1964. His last recordings were for Victoria Spivey's small Chicago label, Spivey Records, that year. His health sank and he stopped recording and performing, then died of heart disease.

Sam was buried in an unmarked grave in a Homewood, Illinois, cemetery. A filmed 2009 concert raised enough money to purchase a headstone for his burial plot.

WASHBOARD SAM

DINAH WASHINGTON

(RUTH LEE JONES)

MAIN INSTRUMENT: Vocals
BORN: Tuscaloosa, Alabama; August 29, 1924
DIED: Detroit, Michigan; December 14, 1963

RECOMMENDED TRACKS: "Evil Gal Blues," "Salty Papa Blues"

Ruth Lee Jones moved to Chicago at age three and at fifteen she won an amateur talent contest with her singing. One of the Sallie Martin Gospel Singers, she played piano and directed her church choir. With her sandpapery, high voice, crisp pronunciation, and bite-sized, blues-tinged phrasing, Ruth rapidly gained a hip following while performing as a nightclub pianist-singer. Lionel Hampton heard about her and asked Ruth to join his band. Hampton claims to have changed Ruth's name to Dinah Washington (she credited Joe Sherman, owner of the Garrick Stage Bar). She sang with Lionel beginning in 1943, with members of Hampton's band supporting her hit solo recording debut that year, "Evil Gal Blues." When she left Hampton in 1946, Washington was already headlining as "the Queen of the Blues."

Dinah's Mercury cover of Fats Waller's "Ain't Misbehavin'," was the first of twenty-seven Top 10 R&B hits from 1948 to 1955. This music included blues as well as pop covers, standards, novelties, and even country (Hank Williams's "Cold, Cold Heart," a 1951 R&B No. 3). "Am I Asking Too Much?" (1948) and "Baby Get Lost" (1949) both reached No. 1. Despite Washington's success in the pop world, she never stopped recording straight jazz, supported by a great roster of players, particularly Clifford Brown on the 1954 live LP *Dinah Jams*. The young Joe Zawinul (later cofounder of Weather Report) backed her on piano for years.

In 1959 Washington made her biggest crossover (No. 4 on the pop chart) into the white market: "What a Diff'rence a Day Makes." She had two hit Brook Benton duets: "Baby (You've Got What It Takes)" and "A Rockin' Good Way (To Mess Around and Fall in Love)," Nos. 5 and 7 on the pop charts, respectively, in 1960. Her last big hit was 1961's "September in the Rain." For the rest of her career, she, like Ray Charles, concentrated on heavily orchestrated ballads. Though she never strayed from her basic vocal approach, critics hated these middle-of-the-road productions.

Dinah was still singing blues in peak form at a club in L.A. just two weeks prior to her death. Her autopsy revealed a lethal combo of alcohol and diet pills.

TRIVIA: Dinah Washington was married seven times. She was a huge influence on singers Nancy Wilson, Esther Phillips, Diane Schuur, and Amy Winehouse.

DINAH WASHINGTON

ETHEL WATERS

MAIN INSTRUMENT: Vocals
BORN: Chester, Pennsylvania; October 31, 1896
DIED: Chatsworth, California; September 1, 1977

RECOMMENDED TRACKS: "Heebie Jeebies," "Am I Blue?," "Down Home Blues,"
"Shake That Thing," "Maybe Not at All," "Black Spatch Blues," "Midnight Blues,"
"Jazzin' Baby Blues"

INTERESTING COVER: "Stormy Weather" (Lena Horne)

Ethel Waters's birth resulted from her mother's rape at age thirteen. Ethel's family was poor and moved a lot, exposing her to music from many cultures. Waters married at thirteen but left her violent spouse to become a Philadelphia hotel maid. Singing at a 1913 Halloween party got her a gig at Baltimore's Lincoln Theatre. Waters toured the black vaudeville circuit, recalling she worked "from nine until unconscious," as quoted in *Current Biography* (1941). She traveled with a carnival, left it in Chicago, and headed to Atlanta, where she found club work, dancing and singing pop songs and ballads, as the blues vocal turf belonged to the club's star, Bessie Smith.

Waters was the fifth black woman ever to record and by 1921 was one of the most powerful entertainers in America. When Fletcher Henderson backed her, she demanded he play "real jazz" with a "damn-it-to-hell bass." Waters hit with "Dinah" and joined a white-audiences-only vaudeville–silent movie combo tour. She cowrote her signature song, "Am I Blue?," in 1929, recorded for major labels throughout the 1930s, and appeared on Broadway. Ethel made the 1933 all-black film spoof *Rufus Jones for President* (with child star Sammy Davis Jr. as Rufus). She was the first black performer in the 1933 Broadway revue *As Thousands Cheer*. Working Broadway while starring in a national radio show as she maintained nightclub gigs made her that era's highest-paid Broadway talent. She reprised her stage role of Petunia in the 1943 MGM hit *Cabin in the Sky*. Her performance in the 1949 film *Pinky* marked the second time an African American was nominated for an Oscar. Waters appeared in the play *The Member of the Wedding*. She made her TV debut starring in the sitcom *Beulah* but quit, as she felt the portrayals of black characters in the show were degrading.

Later in life Waters was robbed of a small fortune in cash and jewelry and hounded by the IRS. Her health declined and work dried up. After her frank autobiography, *His Eye Is on the Sparrow*, she mainly performed for evangelist Billy Graham. Ethel died from cancer of the uterus, kidney failure, and other health complications at the home of the young couple who cared for her.

ETHEL WATERS

MUDDY WATERS

(McKINLEY MORGANFIELD)

MAIN INSTRUMENTS: Guitar, vocals
BORN: Jugs Corner, Mississippi; April 4, 1913
DIED: Westmont, Illinois; April 30, 1983

RECOMMENDED TRACKS: "I Can't Be Satisfied," "Rollin' and Tumblin'," "Rollin' Stone," "Mannish Boy," "She Moves Me," "Hoochie Coochie Man," "I Just Want to Make Love to You," "I'm Ready," "Got My Mojo Working," "You Shook Me"

INTERESTING COVERS: "I Can't Be Satisfied" (Rolling Stones), "Rollin' Stone" (Jimi Hendrix as "Voodoo Chile"), "Hoochie Coochie Man" (Manfred Mann), "I Just Want to Make Love to You" (Foghat), "I'm Ready" (Humble Pie), "Rock Me" (Jeff Beck as "Rock My Plimsoul"), "You Shook Me" (Led Zeppelin), "Got My Mojo Working" (Manfred Mann), "You Need Love" (Small Faces, Led Zeppelin as "Whole Lotta Love")

INTERESTING TRIBUTE: Paul Rodgers recorded *Muddy Water Blues: A Tribute to Muddy Waters.*

As a kid, McKinley Morganfield liked to play in the mud—hence the nickname. His grandmother raised him on Stovall's Plantation in Clarksdale, Mississippi. Muddy's guitar idols were Son House and Robert Johnson. Waters moved to Chicago in 1940, then returned home to run a juke joint. Muddy was first recorded at his home by Alan Lomax in 1941. In 1943 Muddy returned to Chicago, where Big Bill Broonzy helped break him into the club scene.

In 1945 Waters's uncle gave him his first electric guitar. Muddy played with Sunnyland Slim and Eddie Boyd. After one Slim session, Waters recorded two songs, his Aristocrat (later Chess) debut. Once the Chess brothers began recording Muddy in earnest, they wouldn't let the best blues group ever (Muddy's Jimmy Rogers, Little Walter, Elgin Evans, and Otis Spann) in the studio. Like many labels, Chess felt its own session musician pool couldn't be topped. Eventually, the label relented, and Willie Dixon produced a barrage of Muddy Waters blues classics.

The electric volume of Waters's first English gigs in 1958 shocked Brits used to acoustic blues. Muddy's electric *At Newport 1960* live album and acoustic *Folk Singer* LP (1964) helped introduce him to the huge Baby Boomer audience. Johnny Winter reenergized Muddy's fortunes, producing the four bestselling LPs of Waters's career from 1977 through 1981. Muddy's final performance took place in 1982 in Florida, when he sat in with Eric Clapton's band.

TRIVIA: The Rolling Stones took their name from the Waters song "Rollin' Stone." Muddy helped Chuck Berry get his first record contract.

MUDDY WATERS

BUKKA WHITE

(BOOKER T. WASHINGTON WHITE)

MAIN INSTRUMENTS: Guitar, vocals, fiddle
BORN: Near Houston, Mississippi; November 12, 1906
DIED: Memphis, Tennessee; February 26, 1977

RECOMMENDED TRACKS: "Parchman Farm Blues," "Fixin' to Die Blues," "Shake 'Em on Down," "Po' Boy," "Good Gin Blues," "Bukka's Jitterbug Swing"

INTERESTING COVERS: "Fixin' to Die Blues" (Bob Dylan), "Shake 'Em on Down" (Led Zeppelin as "Hats Off to [Roy] Harper")

Booker ("Bukka" was a misspelling of "Booker") White started his career as a fiddler at square dances after learning tunes from his father, who bought him his first guitar. As a teen he befriended blues legend Charley Patton, who helped Booker improve his guitar and women skills.

Spotted by an RCA Victor scout, Booker recorded in Memphis as Washington White in 1930. The Depression kept White from recording until Big Bill Broonzy tipped him to a recording opportunity in 1937. Awaiting trial for shooting a man, Booker jumped bail and recorded two classics ("Shake 'Em on Down" and "Po' Boy") in Chicago before being rearrested. He received three years in Mississippi's infamous Parchman Farm Penitentiary. While doing time, "Shake 'Em on Down" became a hit. A model inmate, Booker recorded in prison as Washington Barrelhouse White for John and Alan Lomax. After his release, he returned to Chicago, ready to record. The 1940 twelve-song session is regarded as Booker's recording peak and includes Delta blues classics "Parchman Farm Blues" (not the Mose Allison "Parchman Farm") and "Fixin' to Die Blues." After that, Booker vanished. The world thought White was dead—but not California blues fans John Fahey and Ed Denson. In 1963 they wrote to "Bukka White (Old Blues Singer), c/o General Delivery, Aberdeen, Mississippi" (from "Aberdeen, Mississippi Blues"). A relative working in the Aberdeen post office forwarded the postcard to Booker in Memphis, where he had been working in a tank factory since WWII. White and Fahey became lifelong friends and Denson, Booker's manager. White studied his 78s and relearned his own songs, performing them at 1960s folk festivals.

By the 1970s, Booker wanted to "go electric" but feared a nasty backlash. White continued playing the folk festivals until his death from cancer.

TRIVIA: White also boxed and played baseball in the Negro Leagues. Booker gave second cousin B.B. King his first guitar, a Stella.

BUKKA WHITE

REVEREND ROBERT WILKINS

(ROBERT TIMOTHY WILKINS)

MAIN INSTRUMENTS: Vocals, guitar
BORN: Hernando, Mississippi; January 16, 1896
DIED: Memphis, Tennessee; May 26, 1987

RECOMMENDED TRACKS: "That's No Way to Get Along," "Rolling Stone"

INTERESTING COVERS: "That's No Way to Get Along" (Rolling Stones as "Prodigal Son," Led Zeppelin reworked as "Poor Tom")

Robert Wilkins was a Cherokee–African American mix. His father was kicked out of Mississippi for bootlegging. His mother married a guitarist who taught Robert guitar. By age fifteen, he was employed at dances and parties. In his early twenties he moved to Memphis with his mother; he stayed there his entire life. Wilkins met Charley Patton and Furry Lewis and claimed he taught guitar to Memphis Minnie. Robert formed a group to profit from the jug band craze but it didn't take off like he expected. He traveled with small vaudeville and minstrel shows and was the first black artist to make a live Memphis radio broadcast.

Vocalion field-recorded eight Wilkins songs at the end of the 1920s, including "That's No Way to Get Along." He later retitled it "Prodigal Son" to capitalize on the success of the Rolling Stones' version (a 1964 ten-minute version Wilkins recorded is a rare masterpiece of extended blues). He recorded alone or with a single accompanist, sometimes as Tim Wilkins or Tim Oliver. In 1935 his life view changed radically. Deeply upset by some violence at a party where he was playing, he left secular music to become a minister in the Church of God in Christ and an herbalist.

Wilkins had never stopped playing, so his chops were better than ever when he was rediscovered by blues enthusiasts who'd simply looked him up in a Memphis phone book. He plugged into the folk festivals, recording and presenting his new blues-tinged gospel to fresh audiences during the 1960s blues revival. Wilkins was nothing if not versatile, a facile player of not just blues and gospel but of ragtime and minstrel songs, too. His grandson wrote his 1995 biography, *To Profit a Man*.

TRIVIA: Early pressings of the Rolling Stones' cover of "That's No Way to Get Along" (as "Prodigal Son") listed the writers as Jagger and Richards, corrected following legal action. The Stones claimed the mistake was the result of the redo of the infamous original *Beggars Banquet* toilet wall cover. Sadly, this didn't result in any royalties for Wilkins, as a Vocalion-connected publisher owned the song's rights.

REVEREND ROBERT **WILKINS**

BIG JOE WILLIAMS

(JOSEPH LEE WILLIAMS)

MAIN INSTRUMENTS: Vocals, guitar
BORN: Crawford, Mississippi; October 16, 1903
DIED: Macon, Mississippi; December 17, 1982

RECOMMENDED TRACKS: "Baby, Please Don't Go," "Crawlin' King Snake"

INTERESTING COVERS: "Baby, Please Don't Go" (Them, AC/DC, Al Kooper)

Young Joe Williams drifted from New Orleans to Chicago, playing streets, bars, work camps—anywhere. In the early 1920s he joined the Rabbit Foot Minstrels revue and in 1930 he sessioned with the Birmingham Jug Band for OKeh Records. In St. Louis record producer Lester Melrose signed him to Bluebird Records, where he stayed from 1935 to '45. In addition to his solo work, he backed other blues singers, including Sonny Boy Williamson I, Robert Nighthawk, and Peetie Wheatstraw.

The guitar and vocal styles of Williams were popular with folk and blues fans throughout the 1950s and '60s. He recorded for a variety of labels and regularly toured the concert, coffeehouse, and festival circuits. He performed throughout Europe and Japan in the late 1960s and early '70s.

Rightfully known as a scrapper (as described in Mike Bloomfield's strange little booklet, *Me and Big Joe*), the smart artists close to Joe treated him as a respected elder statesman of the blues. Few chose to play with him, though; if you played with Big Joe, you had to play by Big Joe's mercurial rules. The "King of the Nine String Guitar" was known for his unpredictable crankiness, but he was also a talented composer, a powerful vocalist, and an incredibly surprising guitarist. More than any other major recording artist, he perfected the guitar-as-drum idea. He beat, tapped, and hammered out an amazing variety of percussive riffs for more than sixty years.

TRIVIA: According to Charlie Musselwhite, he and Big Joe kicked off Chicago's blues revival in the 1960s.

BIG JOE WILLIAMS

ROBERT PETE WILLIAMS

MAIN INSTRUMENTS: Guitar, vocals
BORN: Zachary, Louisiana; March 14, 1914
DIED: Rosedale, Louisiana; December 31, 1980

RECOMMENDED TRACKS: "I've Grown So Ugly," "Prisoner's Talking Blues," "Pardon Denied Again"

INTERESTING COVERS: "I've Grown So Ugly" (as "Grown So Ugly": Black Keys, Captain Beefheart and His Magic Band)

Born into a sharecropping family, Robert Pete Williams picked cotton, cut sugarcane, and never stepped inside a school. At age fourteen he worked in a lumberyard after moving to Baton Rouge. Williams didn't play blues until he was twenty, when he rigged a guitar out of a cigar box and five copper strings. He worked days and practiced nights, then purchased a cheap guitar to play at church gatherings, fish fries, and dances. Despite his hard work, Robert's meager income was such a bone of contention that his wife burned his guitar.

Williams persevered, alternating working the yards and playing dances and juke joints from the 1930s to '50s. In 1956 he shot a man to death in a local club, claiming self-defense. He was convicted of murder and sentenced to life in Louisiana's Angola Prison, the "Alcatraz of the South." Two years in, he was discovered by two musicologists. They recorded Robert's prison songs and begged for his pardon. In 1959 Williams was granted "servitude parole." He received room and board but was virtually prevented from playing music because he had to work eighty hours a week at a Denham Springs farm sans pay. In his first five years out of prison, Williams found time to perform only a few local gigs. His early prison recordings, however, grew in popularity as his great word-of-mouth spread.

In 1964 Williams played at the Newport Folk Festival, his first concert outside Louisiana. Enthusiastically received, he began touring the United States, playing concerts and festivals across America, often with Mississippi Fred McDowell. He toured Europe in 1966 and recorded for several indie labels before settling in Maringouin (near Baton Rouge) and leaving music. He resumed touring American and European festivals in 1970, but cut back by the end of the decade because of his age and deteriorating health.

TRIVIA: Williams's music used unusual blues tunings, patterns, and structures. His lyrics were often about his prison years. He appeared in 1971's *Roots of American Music: Country and Urban Music* and two 1972 French films: *Out of the Blues into the Blacks* and *Blues Under the Skin*.

ROBERT PETE WILLIAMS

SONNY BOY WILLIAMSON I

(JOHN LEE CURTIS WILLIAMSON)

MAIN INSTRUMENTS: Harmonica, vocals
BORN: Near Jackson, Mississippi; March 30, 1914
DIED: Chicago, Illinois; June 1, 1948

RECOMMENDED TRACKS: "Good Morning, Schoolgirl," "Shake the Boogie," "Early in the Morning," "Whiskey Headed Woman Blues," "Sugar Mama Blues"

INTERESTING COVERS: "Good Morning, Schoolgirl" (as "Good Morning Little Schoolgirl": Paul Butterfield Blues Band, Muddy Waters, Grateful Dead, Steppenwolf, Ten Years After), "Sugar Mama Blues" (Taste, Fleetwood Mac).

INTERESTING TRIBUTE: In 2008 protégé Billy Boy Arnold recorded *Billy Boy Sings Sonny Boy.*

Sonny Boy Williamson, "the Father of Modern Blues Harp," is the most important prewar-era harmonica player. He took the humble, country blues–associated support tool and urbanized it into a tough lead instrument. John Lee's vocal-line-followed-by-harp-line call-and-response style has been adopted by nearly every blues harpist.

Hammie Nixon and Noah Lewis were John Lee's harmonica teachers. Williamson drifted and played with Sleepy John Estes and Yank Rachell before putting down roots in Chicago in 1934. In 1937 John Lee's stylistic adaptability and reliable creativity got him signed with Bluebird Records. He recorded frequently, both solo and in support of other Bluebird acts like Robert Lee McCoy (a.k.a. Robert Nighthawk) and Big Joe Williams, who backed John Lee as well. Sonny Boy's first hit was one of his most covered songs, the blues standard "Good Morning, School Girl" (1937). The classics "Sugar Mama Blues" and "Blue Bird Blues" came from that same session. On his "Stop Breaking Down" (1945), the harpist was backed by Tampa Red and Big Maceo. Hugely popular throughout the South and industrial Midwest, Sonny Boy cut more than 120 tracks for RCA from 1937 through 1947, becoming the very first blues harmonica icon.

In 1948 at the peak of his career Williamson was bludgeoned to death during a South Side street mugging as he walked home from what was his final show at the Plantation Club. John Lee's last words were "Lord have mercy."

His last recording, "Better Cut That Out," became a posthumous hit.

TRIVIA: John Lee was so popular that another harp player, "Rice" Miller (see page 210), began using his name in the 1940s, eventually overshadowing the original musician's legacy.

SONNY BOY WILLIAMSON

SONNY BOY WILLIAMSON II

(ALECK FORD, A.K.A. ALECK "RICE" MILLER)

MAIN INSTRUMENTS: Harmonica, vocals
BORN: Sara Jones Plantation, near Glendora, Mississippi; December 5, 1912
(according to census records; 1899 is the birth year most cited,
though other sources say 1897, 1909, or March 11, 1908)
DIED: Helena, Arkansas; May 25, 1965

RECOMMENDED TRACKS: "Bye Bye Bird," "Bring It on Home," "Nine Below Zero,"
"Don't Start Me to Talkin'," "Help Me," "Eyesight to the Blind," "One Way Out"

INTERESTING COVERS: "Bye Bye Bird" (Moody Blues), "Checking Up on My Baby"
(John Mayall's Bluesbreakers), "Bring It on Home" (Led Zeppelin), "Eyesight to the
Blind" (The Who), "One Way Out" (Allman Brothers Band)

Nothing is known of Aleck Ford's early days with his mother and sharecropper
stepfather, Jim Miller. By the 1930s, as Little Boy Blue, he was playing
Delta juke joints, picnics, and even ballgames with partners that included
Robert Johnson, Elmore James, Robert Nighthawk, and Robert Lockwood
Jr. In 1941 he was KFFA's star of *King Biscuit Time*. The Interstate Grocery
Company felt it could sell more King Biscuit flour if Miller posed as Chicago
harmonica star John Lee "Sonny Boy" Williamson. Amazingly, the scam worked,
as their paths never crossed. After John Lee's murder, Miller began calling himself
"the original Sonny Boy."

The live radio show was huge from the start. Sonny Boy cornmeal had Miller's picture on the packaging. Despite his fame, Sonny Boy had little desire to
record. The owner of Trumpet Records eventually tracked Miller down and lured
him into the studio in 1951. He hit with his first release, "Eyesight to the Blind."
When Trumpet went bankrupt in 1955, Chess picked up Miller's contract. Their
first session produced "Don't Start Me to Talkin'," a No. 3 entry on the R&B chart
and his biggest hit. Sonny Boy recorded about seventy songs at Chess.

He toured Europe often during the 1960s British blues mania, recording live
LPs backed by the Yardbirds and the Animals. Sonny Boy headed back to the
States in 1964 for his last Chess sessions, then returned to England as a hero.

In 1965 he came home to Mississippi and resumed the *King Biscuit* show.
Concerned when he missed a broadcast, a search of his rooming house found
Sonny Boy dead in his bed of an apparent heart attack.

TRIVIA: Sonny Boy's "Eyesight to the Blind" is the only song in *Tommy* not written
by any band member of the Who.

SONNY BOY WILLIAMSON

JIMMY WITHERSPOON

MAIN INSTRUMENT: Vocals
BORN: Gurdon, Arkansas; August 8, 1920
DIED: Los Angeles, California; September 18, 1997

RECOMMENDED TRACKS: "Ain't Nobody's Business," "No Rollin' Blues," "Big Fine Girl," "Times Getting Tougher Than Tough"

INTERESTING COVERS: "Ain't Nobody's Business" (Willie Nelson, Freddie King, B.B. King, Sam Cooke, Bobby "Blue" Bland), "Times Getting Tougher Than Tough" (Them), "Big Fine Girl" (Blues Band)

Jimmy Witherspoon sang in a church choir as a child. He gained his first public notice as a vocalist with Teddy Weatherford's band in Calcutta, India. (Teddy made regular U.S. Armed Forces Radio Service broadcasts during WWII.) 'Spoon made his recording debut in 1945 with Jay McShann. Jimmy recorded under his own name in 1949, backed by McShann's band; the result was a No. 1 R&B hit, "Ain't Nobody's Business," which became 'Spoon's signature song.

By the mid-1950s blues shouters were out. Witherspoon released singles for several labels with little success. His LP *Jimmy Witherspoon at the Monterey Jazz Festival* (1959) rejuvenated his career. He toured Europe in 1961, regularly returning to the U.K. thereafter. His best album of the 1960s, *Evening Blues*, featured T-Bone Walker. As the 1970s began, 'Spoon recorded and performed more sporadically. He settled in Los Angeles and worked as a disc jockey.

In 1973 Witherspoon assembled a hot band with a young Robben Ford on lead guitar and hit the road for a successful tour. In London 'Spoon recorded 1975's *Love Is a Five Letter Word* with U.K. blues producer Mike Vernon. Despite a 1980s throat cancer diagnosis, he toured and recorded well into the 1990s. He succumbed to the disease in 1997, keeping active until the end in spite of its effect on his voice.

TRIVIA: In 1971 Witherspoon recorded the underrated album *Guilty* (later released on CD as *Black & White Blues)* with Eric Burdon of the Animals. It features Ike White and the San Quentin Prison Band as backup.

JIMMY WITHERSPOON

JIMMY YANCEY

(JAMES EDWARDS YANCEY)

MAIN INSTRUMENTS: Piano, vocals
BORN: Chicago, Illinois; February 20, 1898 (or 1895)
DIED: Chicago, Illinois; September 17, 1951

RECOMMENDED TRACKS: "The Fives," "Jimmy's Stuff," "Yancey Special"

INTERESTING COVER: "Yancey Special" (Meade Lux Lewis)

Jimmy Yancey worked as a tap dancer and singer in vaudeville beginning at age six. His brother was a pianist, their father a guitarist. Yancey gained real notice as a pianist and by 1915 he was writing songs, playing at parties and get-togethers, and influencing younger guys like Meade Lux Lewis, Pine Top Smith, and Albert Ammons.

Yancey loved baseball. During WWI Jimmy played for the Chicago All-Americans, a Negro league team. In 1925 Yancey began a lifelong career as groundskeeper at Comiskey Park, home of the Chicago White Sox. A musician's musician, Yancey remained a well-kept secret outside of Chicago until 1936, when Lewis recorded Jimmy's "Yancey Special."

Amazingly, Yancey himself never recorded until 1939, when he cut two songs for a small label. His initial recording for RCA Victor was the first collection of boogie-woogie piano solos ever made. After records for OKeh and Bluebird, Yancey performed with his wife, blues singer Estelle "Mama" Yancey; their most celebrated gig was an appearance at Carnegie Hall in 1948.

Yancey, an expressive, sensual musician, wasn't as showy as some of his followers. Instead of being hard-charging, his playing was light and subdued. His limber left hand regularly created surprising bass lines, known as "Yancey bass" to other players, which became the rhythmic backbone for Pee Wee Crayton's "Blues After Hours" and Guitar Slim's "The Things That I Used to Do."

Yancey eventually attained fame for his musical legacy, but he never quit his day job, remaining with his beloved Sox until the day he died from a diabetes-linked stroke.

TRIVIA: Although he wrote and performed compositions in a variety of keys, Jimmy Yancey ended every tune in E flat. After a long solo career, he collaborated with Mama Yancey on the very first album ever made by Atlantic Records.

JIMMY YANCEY

ACKNOWLEDGMENTS

My first expression of gratitude and admiration goes to Robert Crumb, whose endearing *Heroes of the Blues* card set initially inspired my own take on the subject. Denis Kitchen, who published Robert's musical card sets, acted first as my friend and advisor on this project, then expanded his involvement when I asked him to become my agent for this book.

The two original Rhinos, Harold Bronson and Richard Foos, have always supported my work. Harold and I first met because we were both big fans of the Yardbirds. Harold also provides the comfortable setting every couple of months or so for his Musical Cinema Fellowship, whose revolving membership I'd like to thank for their vast (and I mean vast) knowledge, support, and enthusiasm regarding this project. Richard unknowingly sparked this whole adventure when he asked me to draw and paint Mississippi Fred McDowell, J. B. Lenoir and Ma Rainey in the established Crumb trading card format for their Shout! Factory CD covers. Richard and Shout! Factory's Derek Dressler also greatly facilitated the production of this book's CD. And Debbie Brewer, Richard's assistant, is my rock at Shout! Factory: She is always prompt and reliable with her information and help.

Randy Dahlk, my friend and the original designer for this book, continued to help me in every way possible even after he had left the project. My regular publisher, John Fleskes of Flesk Publications, was unhesitant in his cheering and support for this book.

But it's the spouses who suffer most from living with artists. My extremely patient wife, Kent, is no exception; some weekend getaways and two much-needed vacations were canceled because of this book's schedule. Not only did she never complain once, she also made sure that my months of long hours not devoted to her were as pleasant as possible.

It was the LP *Sonny Boy Williamson and the Yardbirds* that really introduced me to my favorite genre of music and started me playing blues harmonica, and for that, I'll be eternally grateful.

My dear friends and longtime fans Patrick Lee and Ed Leimbacher were nothing but enthusiastic about this blues book from the get-go. As soon as I told Pat about this project, he immediately shipped me a huge stack of unreleased live recordings by many of this book's entries, making them available as the potential content for this book's CD (rights issues sadly precluded their use). After agreeing to write this book's introduction, my Big Blues Rock Star Name bailed from the task at the last minute. Asked to pinch hit, Ed stepped up to the plate and hit a game-saving homer with his fine introduction, written with heart and grace in record time. My deepest thanks to these two great guys!

You wouldn't be holding this book without Abrams ComicArts, whose thoroughness and professionalism made my tough but joyful job a lot easier. Charlie Kochman championed this book from his first awareness of it, and Sheila Keenan's terrific editing kept me honest and focused, greatly adding to the text. Designers Chad Beckerman and Sara Corbett were more than patient and never let my picky criticisms dampen their enthusiasm for this book. Thanks to all!

Blue Trimarchi and the great crew at ArtWorks professionally photograph ninety-nine percent of everything I draw and paint and always greet my deadline emergencies with a cheerful can-do attitude. I try not to abuse their time and generosity, but I know I'm not always successful. Thank you!

Thanks to the Brits for waking us up and bringing our own music back to us.

To the musicians (and their bands) in this book whom I saw perform— Chuck Berry, Screamin' Jay Hawkins, Albert King, B.B. King, and Big Mama Thornton—thanks for five incredible shows that thrilled this young white boy to his marrow, and thanks to the concert promoters of the late 1960s who didn't think it was unusual to put British rock groups on the same bill as classic American blues artists. It was my pal Bob Greenberg who introduced me to his friend Screamin' Jay Hawkins. Both have passed, and the world is worse off for their departure. B.B. King showed me that in addition to grit, the blues could have class. Just say "blues" and the Reverend Billy Gibbons of ZZ Top is already on the job, eager to help. I'm looking forward to your contribution to my next book, Billy!

Johnny Otis, whose weekly radio blues show fanned my enthusiastic flames for the genre, informed me and introduced me to many players and singers with whom I was unfamiliar.

George DeCaprio has been my friend and fellow conspirator and collector since the early 1970s. He has never stopped being the same sweet, mischievous guy and passionate supporter of the arts and artists. Here's to that ever-present twinkle in your eyes, George! My friend and fellow artist and Yardbirds fan Al

Gordon has always been able to raise the level of my own enthusiasm for the blues and blues rock with a simple phone call.

California Art Club president Peter Adams immediately provided support in a tangible way by connecting me with Charmaine Jefferson, executive director of the California African American Museum.

Thanks, most of all, to all the blues musicians, past, present and future, who play and sing the blues themselves, often without the proper financial compensation. They have blessed us and continue to stir us with some of the best, most deeply felt music in the world.

BIBLIOGRAPHY

BOOKS

Bogdanov, Vladimir, Chris Woodstra, and Stephen Thomas Erlewine, eds. *All Music Guide to the Blues.* San Francisco: Backbeat Books, 2003

Brooks, Lonnie, Cub Koda, and Wayne Baker Brooks. *Blues for Dummies.* Foster City, CA: IDG Books Worldwide, 1998
This book comes with a twelve-track CD.

Calt, Stephen. *Barrelhouse Words: A Blues Dialect Dictionary.* Urbana and Chicago: University of Illinois, 2009
Ever wonder what it means to "barrelhouse all night long"? You'll find out this (and more) in this fascinating compendium.

———. *I'd Rather Be the Devil: Skip James and the Blues.* Chicago: Review Press, 1994

———. *King of the Delta Blues: The Life and Music of Charlie Patton.* London: Rock Chapel Press, 1988

Charters, Samuel. *Blues Faces: A Portrait of the Blues.* Boston: David R. Godine/Imago Mundi, 2000

Cohn, Lewis. *Nothing But the Blues: The Music and the Musicians.* New York: Abbeville Press, 1993
Great photos, great text—a beautiful book.

Crumb, Robert. *Heroes of Blues, Jazz, and Country.* New York: Abrams, 2006
A wonderful book. These trading card images were the inspiration for this volume.

Davis, Francis. *The History of the Blues: The Roots, the Music, the People.* Cambridge, MA: Da Capo Press, 2003

Deffaa, Chip. *Blue Rhythms: Six Lives in Rhythm and Blues.* Cambridge, MA: Da Capo Press, 2000
Three of the six subjects of this book are blues-related: Charles Brown, Floyd Dixon, and Jimmy Witherspoon.

Dixon, Willie, and Don Snowden. *I Am the Blues: The Willie Dixon Story.* Cambridge, MA: Da Capo Press, 1989

Glover, Tony, Scott Dirks, and Ward Gaines. *Blues with a Feeling: The Little Walter Story.* New York: Routledge, Taylor and Francis Group, 2002

Gordon, Robert. *Can't Be Satisfied: The Life and Times of Muddy Waters.* New York: Little, Brown and Company, 2002

Green, Stephen. *Going to Chicago: A Year on the Chicago Blues Scene.* San Francisco: Woodford, 1990

Guralnick, Peter. *Feel Like Going Home: Portraits in Blues and Rock 'n' Roll.* London: Omnibus Press, 1971
Music history writers don't come better than Peter Guralnick. I'll buy anything this man writes.

Hansen, Barry. *Rhino's Cruise Through the Blues.* San Francisco: Millard Freeman, 2000
Released in conjunction with and to augment Rhino Records' brilliant fifteen-volume CD collection Blues Masters, *this book by the gentleman and music aficionado better known as Dr. Demento is a terrific introduction to the history of the blues.*

Harris, Sheldon. *Blues Who's Who: A Biographical Dictionary of Blues Singers.* New Rochelle, NY: Arlington House, 1979

Harrison, Daphne Duval. *Black Pearls: Blues Queens of the 1920s.* New Brunswick: Rutgers University Press, 1990

Havers, Richard, and Richard Evans. *The Golden Age of The Blues.* New York: Chartwell, 2009
This book comes with a twenty-track CD.

Herzhaft, Gérard. *Encyclopedia of the Blues.* Fayetteville: University of Arkansas Press, 1992

Jones, LeRoi. *Blues People.* New York: Morrow Quill Paperbacks, 1963

King, B.B., and David Ritz. *Blues All Around Me: The Autobiography of B.B. King.* New York: Avon Books, 1996

Mandel, Howard, ed. *The Billboard Illustrated Encyclopedia of Jazz and Blues.* New York: Billboard Books/ Watson-Guptill, 2005
Not quite as encyclopedic as one might wish, this volume is nevertheless an exciting compendium of good writing and great photos regarding the blues.

Obrecht, Jas. *Blues Guitar: The Men Who Made the Music.* San Francisco: GPI Books, 1990

Oliver, Paul. *The Story of the Blues.* London: Barrie and Jenkins, 1970
Despite the muddy reproduction of a lot of its photographs, this important early work is an essential volume that documents the development of the blues.

Palmer, Robert. *Deep Blues.* New York: Penguin Books, 1981
This book has a companion DVD with the same title.

Rolf, Julia, ed. *Blues: The Complete Story.* London: Flame Tree, 2007

———. *The Definitive Illustrated Encyclopedia of Jazz and Blues.* London: Flame Tree, 2007.

Rowe, Mike. *Chicago Blues: The City and the Music.* New York: Da Capo Press, 1986,

Rucker, Leland, ed. *Music Hound Blues: The Essential Album Guide.* Detroit: Visible Ink Press, 1998
Although I have many disagreements with this book tastewise, it contains lots of valuable information within its pages.

Russell, Tony, and Chris Smith. *The Penguin Guide to Blues Recordings.* London: Penguin, 2006
A truly intelligent, informed, and invaluable guide for compiling a superior blues music library. Absolutely essential.

Santelli, Robert. *The Big Book of Blues.* New York: Penguin, 2001 revised and updated edition

Segrest, James, and Mark Hoffman. *Moanin' at Midnight: The Life and Times of Howlin' Wolf.* New York: Thunder's Mouth Press, 2005

Wald, Elijah. *The Blues: A Very Short Introduction.* New York: Oxford University Press, 2010

Wardlow, Gayle Dean. *Chasin' That Devil Music: Searching for the Blues.* San Francisco: Backbeat, 1998
This book comes with a nineteen-track CD collection of early blues recordings.

Wyman, Bill, and Richard Havers. *Bill Wyman's Blues Odyssey.* London: DK Publishing, 2001
A fabulous volume, richly illustrated, thorough yet personal. Don't miss the well-selected two-CD collection on Document Records with the same title.

WEBSITES

www.allmusic.com has a wealth of information about the great blues musicians. This site's biographical material is often written by fellow musicians, who typically add extra musical insight by interpreting or illuminating their subjects and their music.

Wikipedia is also an amazingly good source of information about blues musicians. A lot of work has gone into each entry, with new information being added as it is discovered.

ABOUT THE AUTHOR

WILLIAM STOUT is an award-winning artist and writer who has worked for more than forty-five years in various media, including comics, beginning as an assistant on Russ Manning's *Tarzan of the Apes* and Harvey Kurtzman and Will Elder's *Little Annie Fanny*. He has worked as a designer on more than forty films and on more than 120 film ad campaigns for clients that include Walt Disney, Universal, Jim Henson, Steven Spielberg, George Lucas, Guillermo del Toro, Christopher Nolan, and Monty Python. He is renowned throughout the music industry for his LP and CD covers and has illustrated more than one hundred magazines and books. He is the recipient of the 1992/93 National Science Foundation's Antarctic Artists & Writers Program grant. Stout's prehistoric-life murals are on permanent display at the San Diego Natural History Museum, the Houston Museum of Natural Science, Walt Disney's Animal Kingdom, and the San Diego Zoo. Michael Crichton acknowledged Stout's work as inspiration for *Jurassic Park*. Stout lives in Pasadena, California.

"SATURDAY NIGHT AND SUNDAY MORNING"

BONUS MUSIC CD

COMPILED AND SEQUENCED BY WILLIAM STOUT

❶ Big Joe Williams "Bottle Up and Go" (1:58)
(Traditional; after Tommy McClennan) • Live at Rockford College, 1965

❷ Mississippi Fred McDowell "Jesus Is On the Main Line" (2:14)
(McDowell) • Recorded by Pete Welding and Norman Dayron,
Chicago, Illinois, February 6, 1966

❸ Robert Nighthawk "Kansas City" (2:35)
Recorded at the University of Chicago, Illinois, May 1964

❹ Bukka White "Hot Springs Arkansas" (3:01) (Traditional) • 1974

❺ Robert Wilkins "When I Lay My Burden Down" (3:17) (Traditional) • 1970

❻ Mississippi Fred McDowell "This Little Light of Mine" (2:10)
(Verolja Nix/Traditional) • Recorded by Pete Welding and Norman Dayron,
Chicago, Illinois, February 6, 1966

❼ Bukka White "Mama Don' Low" (3:27) (Traditional) • 1974

❽ Cow Cow Davenport "Cow Cow Blues [instrumental]" (2:38)
(Davenport) • (1928)

❾ Big Joe Williams "Rock Me Mama" (3:02)
(Arthur "Big Boy" Crudup) • Live at Rockford College, 1965

❿ Bukka White "Glory Bound Train" (3:08) (Traditional) • 1974

⓫ Robert Wilkins "Old Time Religion" (4:25) (Traditional) • 1970

⓬ Mississippi Fred and Annie Mae McDowell "Amazing Grace" (3:21)
(John Newton) • Recorded November 24, 1963

BONUS TRACKS:

⓭ Blind Willie McTell "Pal of Mine" (2:42)
(Traditional) • Recorded in Atlanta, Georgia, 1950

⓮ Buddy Moss "Red River" (3:09) (Blind Boy Fuller) • 1966

Total: 41:00

CD compilation ℗ 2012 Shout! Factory LLC
2034 Armacost Avenue, Floor 1, Los Angeles, CA 90025
All rights reserved.

 All of these tracks made available through the generous courtesy of **Shout! Factory**. For a fine selection of more classic blues as well as other great music (and movies), please visit www.shoutfactory.com.
Special thanks to **Richard Foos** and **Derek Dressler** at Shout! Factory.